Contents

Foreword Ashoke Chatterjee		8
Message Jabeen Zacharias		11
Introduction Enter, but with Bowed Head	Jaya Jaitly and Aman Nath	12
Stone New Faces of Permanence	Asha Sairam	16
Glazed Ceramics and Terracotta Shaping What Shapes Us	Kristine Michael	34
Grass, Coir and Natural Fibres Embracing the Planet	Neelam Chhiber	64
Bamboo, Cane and Willow Fresh Breezes Stir Bamboo and Cane	Rebecca Reubens	78
Wood New Roots for Old Trees	A. Balasubramaniam	98
Textiles Flow of Fabric Enters a New World	Jaya Jaitly	124
Surface Decoration Changing the Writing on the Wall	Mitchell Abdul Karim Crites	146
Metal Old Core Gleams Once More	Ayush Kasliwal	176
Glass and Mirror-work Giving Glass a Vanity	Arjun Rathi and Jaya Jaitly	194
Heritage Properties Old Stones Sing Again	Aman Nath	208
Inspiration Enriching a Living Civilization	Jaya Jaitly and Aman Nath	228
Appendices		242

Foreword

This book evokes a memory of a time half a century ago when the notion of interior design as an Indian discipline was just beginning to emerge. A small cohort of design pioneers represented a generation that had tasted freedom and was now eager to express an identity both Indian and contemporary. These pages reveal what a long way that identity has travelled, and what today's achievers might owe to those who helped mould a new nation's sensitivity and taste. Respect for artisans who carry India's heritage in their hands and minds was intrinsic to their awareness of everyday environments and of ways to uplift them. These pages are testimony to how wonderfully that awareness has flourished.

For me, this book is thus an unintended tribute to those who helped prepare the ground for the brilliance celebrated as *Indian Crafts Interiors*. One notes the meticulous listing of all who have come together to create the products and systems which give these interiors their meaning and function. The appendices (offering access to crafts, artisans, organisations, schools, designers and sources of design recognition) are an acknowledgement that is rare yet critical to lifting the handicrafts sector out of misunderstanding and invisibility, moving it towards respect and support as the largest creative resource of its kind in the world. Through astonishing transformations and marriages of tradition, material and technology gathered from every corner of the country, we find heritage and modernity brought together and manipulated towards functional aesthetics that suggest a range of opportunities for tomorrow. Wood, metal and stone find endless combinations. Age-old practices, including those of *sanjhi*, *dhokra* and ritual *kavaad*, move into new expressions and as new materials, enlarging our perception of what is cutting-edge. We are reminded of how to respect nature and of the enduring simplicity that natural materials provide, while Gond and *pattachitra* artists challenge notions of painting, function and scale. A humble lift-shaft transforms into a Madhubani explosion, while the breathtaking achievement at Jaipur's Jal Mahal integrates every sense and every season.

All this is here and much more, suggesting limitless possibilities for innovation, inspiration, research and experimentation. Comprehensive documentation of this quality can inspire and guide students, practitioners, users and all who inhabit spaces that should add value to daily living. Hopefully, this book will encourage further scholarship and innovation, leading to sustained documentation of design achievements, past and present. In a world threatened by climate change and the desperate need for interiors designed for well-being, acknowledgement is overdue of Indian traditions that have for generations transformed the simplest interiors into welcoming and protective environments for ordinary folk with ordinary means. Meanwhile, there is much to learn and celebrate, through what this book offers as "the balance of design when it is open and inspirational" (Jaya Jaitly and Aman Nath, on p. 230). These achievements offer the practice of interiors a new significance, highlighting its potential for quality, livelihood and sustainability. Here is the "many-faceted and many-splendoured fountainhead" that was once an aspiration, now brought to attention through these pages as a brilliant reality of achievement and of promise.

Ashoke Chatterjee
Former Director
National Institute of Design

Message

Handicrafts are the quintessential soul of the Indian interior. The subcontinent and her people have long understood the value of crafts as more than the act of making. Instead, for centuries, crafts have been revered as philosophies, vessels to carry the history of a place and time, and expressions of an unabashed and proud pursuit of beauty. The imprint of crafts on the sands of time is testimony to the thought, skills and ideas that have shaped the exquisite culture of the region.

Modern definitions have often erroneously excluded craft from design, separating the two and relegating the former to a life in the past and the latter to the future. For anyone immersed in studying and creating spaces, this dissociation is a big blunder, one that increasingly paves the way to a certain faceless, "global" homogeneity that erases roots and histories. To be Indian is, and must remain, synonymous with having a privileged and rich relationship with crafts and craftsmen.

In *Indian Crafts Interiors*, The Institute of Indian Interior Designers (IIID) details and celebrates nearly a hundred crafts from India, diverse and especially valuable in the design and curation of spaces and experiences. The book is an important step towards sustaining a curiosity for Indian handicrafts and cementing their place at the helm of Indian interior design, for current and future generations.

The Institute of Indian Interior Designers, founded in 1972, is the apex professional body of designers, architects and related trade personnel in the country. It has a pan-India presence of about ten thousand members spanning 33 Chapters, with its Head Office in Mumbai. IIID plays a vital role in shaping the nation's design policies and trends to suit the changing times and challenges by combating critical design-related issues with visionary responses and campaigns. This book has been published as part of the vision for IIID's 2019–21 term "Where is North?", which signifies conscious and conscientious design for a better tomorrow.

Jabeen Zacharias
President (2019–2021)
Institute of Indian Interior Designers

INTRODUCTION

Enter, but with Bowed Head

• Jaya Jaitly and Aman Nath

The "wonder" that was India is still the great wonder that India is! Especially if one sets aside any arrogance or condescension while arriving at the doorstep of a craftsperson. An encyclopaedic knowledge linked to craft skills and an awareness of all the nuances and unpredictability of their materials still lives on, intuitively awake and instinctively drilled into their DNA. After all, India is the world's only civilization, of its scale, to remain continuously alive through the millennia. Other ancient cultures, which began some three millennia later, also ended much earlier than ours because they had built false social momentums geared only to power, greed and materialism. Having not understood the ephemeral in life, the Egyptians even put objects in the sarcophagi for use in the afterlife, while we turn life effortlessly to ash and mingle it with the eternal elements of fire, earth and water.

The most remarkable aspect of India's craft skills and their practitioners is their adaptability to engage with and enhance the work of contemporary designers who wish to make their creative output both aesthetic and uniquely Indian. The term "designer" applies here not merely to architects and interior designers but to fields as widespread as tourism, graphic design, fashion, and intermediate and appropriate technology, and can play a strong part

A large ritual bell metal lamp takes pride of place in the home of the maker.
Image credit: Dastkari Haat Samiti

in the combination of economic and cultural oases. Unlike heavily industrialized countries, more than one hundred craft skills are still alive in India, and, when infused with aspiration and accessibility into modern environments, they are thriving and continuously morphing, often in the hands of able professionals in urban design offices and studios everywhere.

From a predominantly agrarian society, India is slowly changing and layering, rather than discarding, its old ways of organic farming and manual work, even modernizing traditional wisdom in health and medicine through technology and science. The beliefs that natural indigo dyes are good for the skin or that turmeric is a textile colourant as well as an anti-inflammatory agent in food or that, altogether, natural dyes are better for the environment—are being readily accepted internationally. Traditionally, Indian women are experts at recycling, renovating and repurposing. Their quilting of frayed fabrics in *kantha*s has become an art form, transforming a simple coverlet into a storytelling spread in fine embroidery, the aesthetics of which designers often cannot match. These constitute a valuable knowledge base that can transform the world of design. Particularly in the use of natural materials in the interiors, India's rural structures employ a mixture of clay and lime, while larger palaces and forts have been generous with stone, which acts as a cooling agent in desert areas, with lattices further allowing in breeze. Narrow, shallow water channels ran along corridors to provide a cooling system. Contemporary architecture and interiors in Kerala and Goa employ many old techniques in brick, tile and wood, with elements of old balconies as a tribute to a fast-disappearing culture. Even the burnished lime walls, *araish*, or floors made with crushed eggshells in the mix, make sporadic appearances.

Earlier, crafts skills were employed in interiors of homes to provide many necessary elements of utility. Care needs to be taken today to not make these merely decorative because, in India, any crafted object or aspect of an interior environment has always had a deeper meaning, whether practical or ritualistic. The Indian-ness would become superficial and hollow if designers ignored this aspect.

In Karnataka, there is a craft skill in which rosewood is carved and inlaid with patterns, often comprising up to 45 different types of wood, such as mango, jackfruit and rubber, etc. Coconut wood is being used by contemporary architects as outer wall cladding or shutters. Mango wood, which is one of the easiest to obtain, is now being processed through technology to make good quality furniture. Similarly, natural materials such as jute and a variety of other wild and cultivated grasses today provide inspiration for cooling partitions and wall cladding. Indian interior designers have great opportunities now to offer truly eco-friendly, cost-effective, natural environments for comfort, ecological and aesthetic reasons, with the added rare element of locally available hand skills.

The crafted elements that are unique to India and some South Asian countries offer the true meaning of "bespoke" in any field of design because they can make the client feel special and pampered. While each interior is differently imagined according to the interaction between the interior designer and the client, when this is enriched through the third element, of a craftsperson interacting intimately with the designer, the palette of possibilities increases. All designers chase innovation, and this is most achievable when working with skilled craftspeople.

Handmade tiling for floors, textures for surfaces or furniture, custom-woven textiles, lamps individually fashioned out of pliable bamboo or even handmade paper: these are

Introduction • 13

all innovations that can happen more easily in the handmade sector and for individual interiors that do not need a large number of units to be economically viable. The amount paid to the craftsperson sustains an average family unit of five for months, which adds an extra level of satisfaction. But it isn't easy to ensure any continuity of demand, even for master craftspeople, putting the sustenance of their families in jeopardy. The death knell of any craft strikes when the next generation is lured away by the easy security and magnetism of urban offices. The civilizational abacus is falsely seen to be illiterate against the laptop glitz of soulless, glass-enclosed cubicles.

International design journals have an expected repetitive quality about them. Glass and steel, faux leather, monochrome colour palettes and meaningless abstractions on the walls are a common aesthetic. Most settings are pristine and seem not to hold much life. This is perhaps because these journals are heavily supported by major international companies that supply bathroom fittings, rugs, kitchen units and glass. In comparison, Indian designers can instantly adorn any room with voluptuous colours on walls, tables, cushions, and any remaining space with tropical plants. The vibrancy and variety of life seem to burst forth. This is what tourists come to find in India. Our public spaces, tourist resorts and hotels have the greatest options in the world to offer multiple cultural expressions through the hands of our craftspeople, combining with the sophisticated contemporary sensibilities of interior designers and architects of today.

To understand the power of the continuous design thought or the eternal in India, enter an educated, current-day "designer" into the home of an *ikat* weaver working on his loom on the eastern coast of India. Give the designer all the thread and dyes at hand as also a crash course on how the hand-spun thread on the spinning wheel is stretched and dyed in advance and then carefully preserved in the inherited wisdom cradled in the master craftsman's mind to become a peacock, the *annam* or a seaside conch. The weaver has to plan the design to be woven well in advance. The threads stretched across the loom are

A textile craftsman in Gujarat prepares the warp thread on a vibrant piece of fabric.
Image credit: Mapin

divided carefully according to the proposed proportions of the design on the body of the finished piece. The entire piece has to be imagined well before execution. There can be no second thoughts. Knots are tied at intervals where the colour of the dye has to change. After the knots along the full length are tied, the weft is woven in to create the motifs and complete the pre-conceived layout. To imagine and then to translate into reality a fabric where the real magic lies in the plan as well as the tying and dyeing, and not the actual weaving, is hard to grasp for a layperson. Let the designer try out the educated hand, linked to a literate, computer mind, to shuttle through the warp and weft of ignorance, if one may say so, to be humbled to contemporary dust. This is Indian craft for us all: reverentially quiet as the *garbha griha* of a temple, modest yet mind-blowing, riddled in its own economic poverty but rich enough to be never counted in a rustle of fresh banknotes. This process can be repeated at the workplace of all Indian craftspeople who sit confident in their own arenas. This demands humility.

Every form in Indian civilization has evolved with centuries, if not millennia, of usage and refinement between the user and the creator. Craftspeople aware of the strengths and limitations of their materials, climatic concerns and other constraints have mastered and steered their practices through many a storm. The storms now blow again, and many of them are reinventing themselves, with new designs and innovations, to stay afloat while still observing the rules of their practices. This book will feed the fertile minds of today's creative people and, we hope, continue this process. •

STONE

New Faces of Permanence

STONE

New Faces of Permanence

• Asha Sairam

Stone is central to the architectural heritage of the Indian subcontinent, having been used as a construction material in this context for millennia. The earliest examples of Indian stone architecture are recognized to this day as outstanding feats of human achievement, like the *chaitya* halls and *vihara*s carved onto stone at Ajanta and Ellora. In later centuries, additive stone structures in the form of *stupa*s, temples and palaces began to take shape, choosing not to merge into their landscapes like their subtractive counterparts, but to stand as markers in space, symbolizing the values of their time.

The use of stone in Indian architecture has contributed to timeless architectural marvels through the ages, but it has also left an intangible imprint through craft traditions that continue to this day. Each region has its own heritage of stone crafts arising from local material resources, along with communities of skilled craftspeople. Because of this, the Taj Mahal could only have been built in Agra or its surrounding regions—due to their proximity to *makrana* marble sources and artisan communities well versed with stone use in Rajasthan. Similar associations can be made between the Konark Temple in Odisha and the state's laterite and khondalite reserves, and between Madhya Pradesh's iconic Khajuraho Temples and its sandstone mines. Thus, a common characteristic emerges among these stone monuments from different historical periods: they are all expressions of material resources and skills unique to their regions, making them rooted in their context and thus inherently sustainable.

Today's built environments are a far cry from these examples. In our hyper-globalized world, we carry a homogenized set of aspirations, which are then projected onto the buildings we build—

so much so that a building in Gurugram starts to resemble one in New York or Hong Kong. These buildings disregard the profuse diversity of our country's culture, climate, and geography, following benchmarks that belong to contexts vastly different from ours. As a result, our social and ecological systems are under threat, with a culture of thoughtless consumption taking its place, which is decimating our natural resources and putting local communities at risk. We've been looking up to the wrong paradigms all along. What is the right benchmark then?

The values of Studio Lotus evolved as a response to this question. We began looking inwards, examining advanced building systems that have existed in India for millennia and searching for answers within the deep recesses of vernacular wisdom. Our work is an ongoing engagement to understand the places we build in and the people we build for, resulting not only in spaces that respond to their context but also in frameworks that are appropriate for their context.

Our experiments with stone are an expression of these core values—principles that we believe must be addressed by contemporary Indian architecture. From redefining luxury and making the local aspirational, to frugal innovation and doing more with less, to contemporizing age-old building traditions and crafts, our beliefs take physical form through explorations of the myriad qualities of stone—its tactility and flexibility, its resilience and translucence.

Celebrating Context: Making the local aspirational

A hospitality project set in the foothills of the Himalayas, RAAS Kangra is an experiment in making vernacular traditions synonymous with luxury, influencing local aspirations to move away from imported materials. The building's

PREVIOUS PAGES
Sculpting waves in stone.
Image credit: PMA Madhushala

walls are built in stacked stone masonry similar to that found in rural houses in Himachal Pradesh, using waste slate from local quarries. The thick masonry walls envelop the hotel with high thermal mass, retaining internal heat and protecting it from Kangra's cold weather. Slate stone and timber combine to form a building that gently emerges from the site and exemplifies the simplicity and harmony of Kangra's Buddhist monasteries. The indigenous architectural vocabulary of the region is given a new expression, with local materials used to craft an atmosphere of understated luxury.

While the RAAS Kangra rendered vernacular building materials aspirational by making them synonymous with luxury, Krushi Bhawan in Bhubaneswar does so by introducing them into an accessible public building. A facility for the State of Odisha's Department of Agriculture and Farmers' Empowerment, Krushi Bhawan subverts the traditional image of a government office as an impenetrable and high-security building. Instead, a porous, landscaped realm on the ground floor opens up the building's site to the public, returning a significant portion of it to them as a space for repose, learning and collaboration.

Laterite was the primary material used in the stilted space; a locally available stone that is easy to carve, it transformed the plaza's walls into a canvas for local artisans. *Bas-reliefs* depicting paddy crops and other agricultural scenes are engraved into these walls, illustrated in the Odia *pattachitra* style of art. Khondalite is also used to create ribbed columns evocative of Odisha's temples and hand-carved stone screens with floral motifs. By celebrating crafts and local materials, Krushi Bhawan fosters a sense of familiarity, belonging and ownership among its visitors and daily users. Vernacular traditions are built into people's aspirations through their integration in a government building—one that is an accessible civic institution and a symbol for the city (See, pages 30–31).

Contemporizing Craft: New narratives for age-old traditions

RAAS Jodhpur, developed in collaboration with the Bengaluru-based firm Praxis Inc., is a property steeped in centuries of history, with an ancient stepwell lying to its south and the 15th-century Mehrangarh Fort rising to its west. Completed in 2010, the hotel acts as a portal between the past and the present by reinterpreting a timeless building element for the modern age—the *jaali*.

The sandstone *jaalis* of RAAS Jodhpur are contemporary derivatives of the double-skinned structures of Rajasthan. Designed to provide

The traditional *jaali* is given a contemporary expression at the RAAS Jodhpur by creating a lantern-like, foldable double skin using sandstone panels, developed with skilled local masons.
Image credits: Noughts & Crosses LLP, Andre J Fanthome

passive cooling, ventilation and privacy, they are the handiwork of nearly a hundred local artisans, taking shape from numerous trials of patterns, techniques and panel dimensions. Stone screens, each of 18 mm thickness, form a sliding-folding system, allowing visitors to open up the *jaali*s to expansive views of the fort. On other walls, 50 mm-thick panels carved with the same patterns shield interior spaces from heat, allowing light to filter through. The handicraft traditions of Jodhpur's artisans, passed down to them through generations, shape an entirely new response in stone. Tradition is contemporized at RAAS Jodhpur: the handmade is augmented by technology and merged with modern sensibilities.

The property is also the result of a collaborative design process, where the iterative and trial-and-error methods of traditional handicrafts shaped the final building. While an overarching vision determined its output, the involvement of artisans gave a handmade touch to the building, imbuing it with the spirit of the place. The utilization of local skills and resources in its design and construction gave a fillip to the artisanal industries of the city, reviving the craft ecosystems of the region and making them relevant and accessible to a new generation.

Frugal Innovation: Doing more with less

While RAAS Jodhpur features sandstone in the form of a screening element, the Mehrangarh Fort Visitor Centre, under construction nearby, uses it as an optimized building block. Insulated sandstone panels engraved with various patterns are designed to create an envelope, consuming only a third of the material used by a standard stone masonry wall. Traditional craftsmanship is integrated with a kit-of-parts construction strategy that employs dry construction methods, creating a modular, woven steel frame that allows the building to adapt to future needs. In this manner, the Visitor Centre incorporates locally sourced materials in a frugal manner that is appropriate to the modern age in which such resources are limited.

Although stone is usually celebrated for its weight and monumentality, the central pavilion at the Baradari restaurant in Jaipur expresses an unconventional quality of the material. Twelve slender marble columns hold up a mirrored roof, in an ode to traditional 12-pillared Rajputana pavilions. Brass inlays and backlighting further accentuate the lithe profiles of the columns, rendering the pavilion as a lightweight and airy intervention to

Set in the heart of the walled city of Jodhpur, Rajasthan, RAAS is a 1.5-acre property located at the base of the Mehrangarh Fort. The drama of the stone *jaali* here is heightened by the fact that these panels can be folded away by each guest to reveal uninterrupted views of the fort, or can be closed for privacy and to keep the harsh Jodhpur sun out.
Image credits: Noughts & Crosses LLP, Andre J Fanthome

LEFT
The existing buildings at the Baradari, a remodelled museum café and restaurant, were given a new expression by repairing the exposed rubble masonry with traditional lime mortar, with details formed in lime plaster.
Image credit: Studio Lotus

RIGHT
The restaurant's North Verandah after restoration.
Image credit: Edmund Sumner

its compact surroundings. Stone takes on a novel expression here, becoming delicate and translucent, almost invisible.

The Way Forward: Using stone in contemporary buildings

Today, architects stand at a crucial juncture in history. We carry an intrinsic consciousness of our traditions and culture, along with a sound understanding of contemporary sensibilities and the best of today's technology. What we choose to do with this diametric knowledge will determine the future of our built environment.

As inheritors of a heritage of building that is as old as time itself, we have a greater responsibility to ensure that these crafts don't disappear into obscurity, adapting them so that they remain relevant for present times. Modern architecture should explore new and inventive ways of incorporating and contemporizing traditional crafts and artisanal skills.

India's building traditions emerge from a profound understanding of the climate and culture of a place, evolving through centuries of wisdom. When integrating them into modern-day buildings, their fundamental sustainable principles must be accounted for and respected, so that they don't remain merely superficial gestures. The above examples used certain materials because they were available locally and could be sourced near the site. Incorporating the sustainable response underlying vernacular traditions makes for a holistic and well-rounded response to context and local culture—one that combines both symbol and purpose.

These traditions do not exist in isolation but as part of a larger ecosystem of skilled artisans and industries. The design process must also engage these diverse stakeholders and be shaped by their inputs, with the architect acting as a mediator in an emergent and collaborative approach. These varied perspectives and skill sets inform the final product, with artisans who improvise their craft in a dialectic approach, tuning into the architect's vision, much like a *jugalbandi*. •

Stone

Natural stones can be used in a variety of ways for both interior and exterior purposes, such as aesthetics, structural solutions, flooring and surface treatment. Stone is greatly valued for timelessness and is a classic material that can make any space look more elegant and luxurious. Flooring is done using a combination of locally available stones of different quality and hardness to achieve interesting and colourful compositions. Surface treatment is done by either carving or cladding the surface with stones of different patterns and colours. Techniques include cutting, carving and polishing of stones, which is achieved manually or through machines.

Inspiration: The idea of sustainable and traditional design processes inspired us to use stone craft in numerous projects. Traditional houses and *haveli*s display beautifully carved columns, niches, brackets and various other elements. These elements have been contemporized in a coherent manner in an attempt to meet the agelessness of traditional architecture.

Sustainability: Designing with stone presents an exciting array of options. Moreover, natural stones are durable and their process of installation is harmless to the environment. Establishing the use of stone craft in designing processes ensures the continuity of this traditional method and the survival of the skills of the craftsmen, which have been passed down for generations. ∎

Material: Granite, limestone, sandstone, marble, slate, gneiss, serpentine
Technique: Carving, cutting, grinding and polishing
Source Region: Gujarat and Rajasthan, India
Studio: Abhikram Architects, Panika Crafts and Technologies

Stone

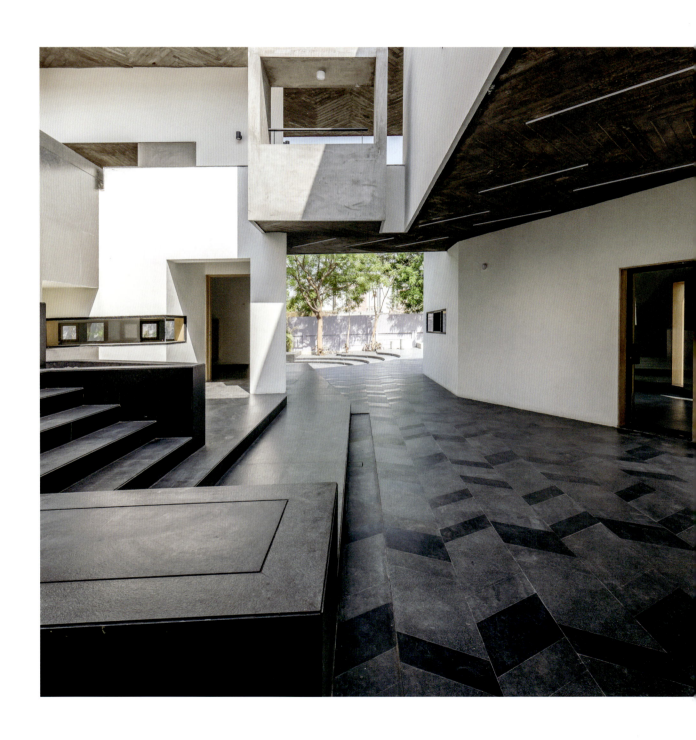

Black granite of three finishes (honed, leather-finished and rough) was used in this project. In gallery spaces, large, leather-finished blocks were used to create a calm surface, tying the space together. In the circulation areas, the central courtyard and the amphitheatre, different finishes were used to create a vibrant, patterned mosaic. The stone was treated by brushing, polishing, hammering and application of heat and water. They were cut and assembled on site.

Inspiration: Being a publicly accessible building that sees a lot of footfall, it needed a flooring of good durability. Granite, being dense, impermeable to water and stain resistant, made it an ideal choice. Since granite is also locally available, transportation of the material was not an issue, and the ability to use different finishes gave us a lot of possibilities to create attractive patterns.

Sustainability: Granite is locally available, so there is no carbon footprint with respect to transportation. Given its great durability, it is also long-lasting and requires very little maintenance. ■

Material: Granite
Technique: Black granite stone cut on site as per the design and cast in a grey cement base, while others are used to form textured patterns.
Source Region: Rajasthan, India
Studio: Studio Sangath

Stone

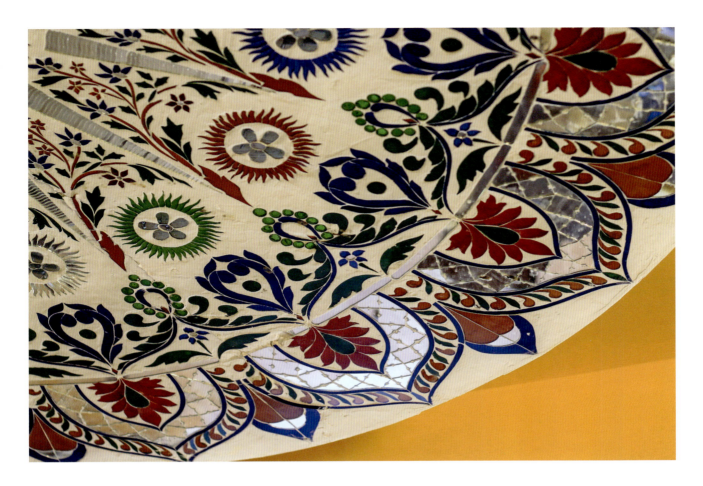

*P*ietra dura is a term for using cut and fitted, highly polished coloured stones to create images. The term signifies the requisite hardness and durability of the materials used in this work. The stonework is glued stone-by-stone to a base after being sliced and cut in different shape sections. It is then assembled together so precisely that the contact between each section is practically invisible.

Inspiration: Rajasthan, also known as the Land of Rajputs, is noted across the globe for its art, crafts, culture, palaces and forts. The ancient history of Rajasthan demands the advocacy and patronage of all the great art forms of the state, albeit by giving them a contemporary touch.

Sustainability: The stone and precious gems are responsibly sourced and worked on by traditionally trained artisans, who are able to minimize waste. The surfaces thus decorated are easy to clean and maintain over long periods of time. ∎

Material: Stone, precious gems
Technique: Inlay
Source Region: Rajasthan, India
Studio: Somaya & Kalappa Consultants

Stone

Inspired by traditional Maharashtrian stone-working techniques, the stone used here was surrendered to local artisans to excavate its ancestral handmade rawness. They shaped stones with simple tools called *sutki*, *chinni* and *woordi*, generating various finishes, such as *bouch* (rough), *tichiv* (granular), *sajguri* (finer) and *mativ* (finest). Thereafter, local styles of construction and specifications such as *tachkali* (grooveless joints), *khaandki* (ashlar) and *kali* (random rubble) were adopted and customized into the design.

Inspiration: Over thousands of years, the local stone (basalt) has given an identity to the local architecture and has, therefore, become a token of timelessness, weathering in its natural pace. Functioned to bear heavy loads, a rigid material like this can bind with time, technology and creativity to showcase innumerable variants of a conventional purpose.

Sustainability: Based in the lands of hard basalt boulders, the site became the direct source of raw material. It was then worked on with traditional, non-industrial techniques, thus promoting the ancestral crafts of the local communities. The residual waste of the stonework was utilized as infill, making the built environment a stone depository for future use. ■

Material: Basalt stone
Technique: Traditional stonework
Craftsperson(s): Dhyaneshwar Dhotre
Source Region: Maharashtra, India
Studio: PMA Madhushala

Stone

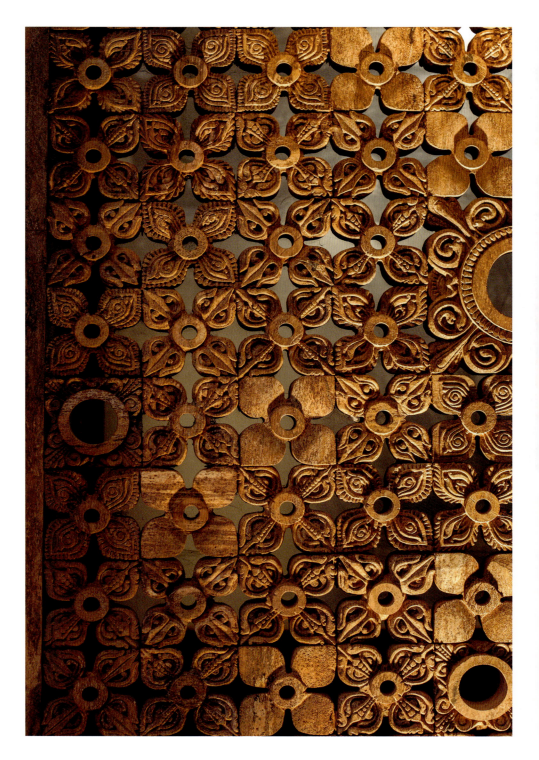

Krushi Bhawan, in Bhubaneswar, is a public building designed for the Department of Agriculture, Government of Odisha. A craft programme was developed to include the work of traditional artisans in the building. An approach blending contemporary design with traditional craftsmanship ensured synergy in the artisanal work and the building. Locally sourced laterite and khondalite (sandstone) were used, and local artisans who have extensive experience in stone carving were employed to demonstrate the richness of the crafts of Odisha.

Inspiration: The inspiration was drawn from the rich tradition of stone carving in Odisha, a highly developed tradition due to the age-old practice of building elaborate temples in the region. Owing to this, there exists in the region a large pool of talented stone carvers and artisans, who were employed here in a contemporary setting.

Sustainability: Locally sourced stone reduced the environmental burdens on the project. Further, the application of traditional stone craft in a contemporary setting resulted in the creation of a unique design idiom, as well as equipping the artisans with greater skills and generating employment. ■

Material: Sandstone, metal
Technique: Stone carving, *pattachitra* painting, wrought-iron crafts
Source Region: Odisha, India
Studio: Studio Lotus, in collaboration with Sibanand Bhol, Collective Craft

Stone

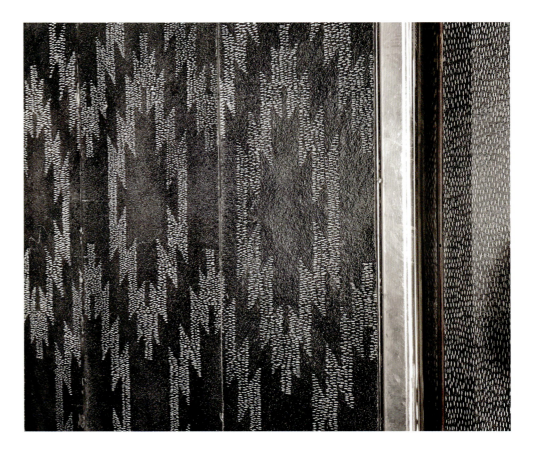

This project was envisioned to demonstrate the mainstream application of crafts, within the decided budget and timelines, for corporate branding, vision and design. Craftspeople in Rajasthan are famous for their inlay and etching work on stone and wood. Vibrant geometric motifs, evoking the designs on sari borders, were etched into the stone flooring and wooden elements, offering a direct design experience to the customers. Local cuddapah stone was sourced for this project to enhance the core vision of sustainability and artisanship, while also reflecting the brand values.

Inspiration: Since the shop was a boutique apparel outlet, with beautiful saris, the designs on the sari borders became the inspiration for the inlay and etching work on the stone and wooden elements. Various geometric motifs were created to reflect the beauty of the products on display; the fact that these patterns were on the stone flooring or wooden tables further enhanced the impression of organic design.

Sustainability: The use of non-industrially produced materials, made by hand or with simple tools, and the full recyclable nature of this retail design is the main aspect of sustainability here. Moreover, most of these crafts deliver the best with minimum carbon footprint. There is also the creation of employment, which directly benefits the local economy, and the skill development of craftspeople is another advantage of this approach. ■

Material: Stone, wood
Technique: Inlay and etching
Craftsperson(s): Raghav/Dhoot Sangemermer (DSPL), Jaipur (wood inlay), Gopi/Monolith Granites
Source Region: Rajasthan, India
Studio: Dustudio

Stone

This project involved the clever use of stone in such a way that the niches cut into the stone slabs become a part of the brick-stone narrative. Stone was used in its authentic form throughout the building. A cutting machine was used to cut the stone wherever required, but other than that cement acted as the binding agent. This design solution was executed in accordance with the principles of vernacular architecture, where local materials and resources are used without any additional investment, thereby reducing waste to a minimum. The white sandstone was quarried from the Dhangadhra mines located in Surendranagar, in Gujarat, and masons from Saurashtra, also in Gujarat, were involved in the construction of this building.

Inspiration: The most fascinating aspect of this craft is that the strength of the wall is maintained, while providing an aesthetic play to the surface. Depressions and protrusions are created without changing the predominant course of stone. Furthermore, the rough texture of stone combined with brick creates an unconventional design narrative.

Sustainability: The stone used is strong, porous, durable and locally available. There was also the aspect of social sustainability in the revival of an age-old craft in contemporary architecture and the skill development of the artisans involved. ■

Material: White sandstone
Technique: Cutting
Craftsperson(s): Jitubhai, Sailesh, Ramnikbhai
Source Region: Gujarat, India
Studio: D6thd Studio

GLAZED CERAMICS AND TERRACOTTA

Shaping What Shapes Us

GLAZED CERAMICS AND TERRACOTTA

Shaping What Shapes Us

● Kristine Michael

Haku Shah's celebrated exhibition *Form and Many Forms of Mother Clay* (*Maati, Ye Tere Rup*) at the Crafts Museum, New Delhi, in 1983, was dedicated to Lord Prajapati, Pupul Jayakar and Stella Kramrisch, the authorities of creation, modernity and art history, respectively. It was the first major exhibition on the craft of the Indian potter and the embedded, integral part it had played in Indian society, both urban and rural. Conscious of the destructive repercussions that rural crafts and culture faced with post-Independence modernity, the exhibition gave us an imagining of the intersection that pottery played in life in India in the past—the intertwining of relationships between the material, sustainable production technologies and demand systems, the sustenance of daily life, ritual and spirituality.

Very little remains of that agrarian context today as there are many challenges facing traditional potters. Khamir-SETU conducted a study in 2014 on the work status of potters, with a survey of 145 potters' families from 54 villages across Kutch. The key challenges faced are firstly that of shrinking clay sources: there is encroachment by farmers, property developers, industries and traders as well as increasing pollution due to the dumping of industrial and urban waste. Secondly, compared to other craft artisans, potters have not seen much upgradation in their work facilities, tools and equipment. Due to lack of adequate work sheds, pottery practice often comes to a halt during monsoons. In most urban cities, potters have to work in cramped conditions, facing hostility from their neighbours due to the processes of their work, especially firing. Thirdly, there is a generational shift in occupation due to low

financial returns, which means that many of the younger family members do not want to get involved any more. Pottery practice is hard work that requires the involvement of the entire family in a household-based activity. Furthermore, with dwindling local markets, the return in value for the effort put in is unsustainable. Even though Khadi and Village Industries, development organizations, design schools, traders and NGO groups assist with product design and the development of new markets, new technologies in glazing and firing with some pottery clusters, the profit margin remains low, and existence is still almost hand-to-mouth for most.

The versatility of this medium makes it ideal for both interiors and the landscaping of external spaces. Viewers experience the tactile, colourful and emotive nature of the material. The tropes of a rural craft in transition as well as the romanticization of a past lifestyle, which is integral to our cultural memory, are strong encouragement for the continued interest and fascination with the material. This essay aims to give an insight into some of the various ways in which both unglazed terracotta and glazed ceramics have been used most effectively by designers, artists and the craftsmen themselves in making it relevant to the needs of the 21st century.

Working with clay, one of the oldest materials known to mankind, is the most sustainable, owing to the simplicity of the technology of making and firing for permanence. Clay is available all over the country; malleable; easy to work with; and endowed with remarkable qualities of porosity, thermal properties, fire

PREVIOUS PAGES
A detail from the mural at Amigo Securities in Vadodara by P.R. Daroz.

LEFT
A free-standing monumental sculpture at the Hyatt Hotel in Chennai by Ray Meeker.
Image credit: Ray Meeker

RIGHT
Women painting clay utensils. Painting is done using either a small bamboo tool, beaten at one end to form a frayed end, like a brush, or with the end of a shred of cloth tied to a twig. Decoration is based on geometric patterns with abstract stylizations of human, animal and floral motifs.
Image credit: Anand Patel

resistance and longevity. Building with sun-dried earth blocks, or the use of terracotta bricks or decorative panels (such as those in the medieval terracotta temples in Bengal), has long been an important feature in vernacular architecture. The contemporary use of the plastic and dynamic qualities of this material in modern architecture, in both internal and external spaces, has been explored by many. For example, Laurie Baker of Trivandrum developed and applied a low-cost approach to housing, derived from an intimate understanding of the local climate, available building materials and craft skills, as well as the detailed attention to the specific needs of his individual clients. He influenced the resource-intensive architecture prevalent by pruning all non-local materials. His inventive usage of un-plastered local bricks and clay tiles to create window openings through patterns of *jaalis*, or lattices, in the brickwork, thus providing adequate light, ventilation and security, was revolutionary in modern post-Independence architecture.

Design development in terracotta interior products for artisanal support, with potters from Nepal as well as Pondicherry, was done by Ray Meeker of Golden Bridge Pottery in his fired, stabilized building technology project. The experimental project postulated that the village potter whose livelihood was under threat and whose knowledge and skill were no longer fully utilized held great potential for creating a rural clay-based industry. Stretched over a period of 20 years, it was seen that practically the whole dwelling system could be made in terracotta—both glazed and unglazed—including burnished floor tiles, *jaali* screens and murals, earthenware toilets, cutwork lanterns and lamp bases, roofing *guna* tiles, stools with glazed seats, hanging planters and smokeless *chulhas*.

Gurcharan Singh at Delhi Blue Art Pottery took the concept of the perforated screen further with his glazed copper-blue tessellation module unit and tiles that were widely used in the buildings of New Delhi in the mid-20th century by architects such as Joseph Allen Stein, B. V. Doshi, Dr. J. R. Bhalla and Habib Rehman. Other ceramic artists such as P. R. Daroz and Ray Meeker have created large-scale free-standing ceramic doorways or archways as landscape

Glazed Ceramics and Terracotta • 37

features, often near water bodies, reminiscent of excavations or archaeological ruins.

Many potter communities have transitioned to making both objects for the customary festival, ritual and functional purposes as well as adapting to urban commercial needs, public buildings and social media platforms. The interventions of J. Swaminathan of Bharat Bhawan, Bhopal, and Jyotindra Jain of the Crafts Museum, Delhi, were some of the first to acknowledge and validate the making of art by the individual traditional or vernacular artist, instead of a homogenizing rubric that upheld the trope of the anonymous craftsman. This essay highlights some examples of this transition from the vernacular, in order to show not only the range and versatility of the medium in public and private spaces but also the design facilitation efforts to create a new market economy for the craft of pottery.

The Molela potters' group, led by Dinesh Chandra Kumhar, was commissioned by the Rajasthan state government to make the façade of the Udaipur Railway Station building in 2006. They used their traditional style of hollow relief for clay figures on the flat surface of the plaque to narrate stories of the deity Dharmaraj. However, in the contemporary versions of the Molela plaques, they comment on city life, imbuing it with wonder and sharp wit—people riding cycles, travelling by train, schoolchildren with rucksacks, and other observations—in a natural clay finish. Normally, the plaque is then painted using organic pigments and lac, but it can also retain its distinctive natural earth-red colour surface.

Ceramic artists, such as Vadodara-based fine arts graduate Jagruti Dutta, continue with the large terracotta tile or plaque format with detailed relief work based on the theme of nature. Coming from a farming background, Dutta attempts to capture the beauty of the transitory nature of seasonal change, the impermanence and the wonder in a medium close to her heart and hands. The combination of the flying birds breaks the rigidity of the tiles, giving the illusion of upward or diagonal movement.

Vibrantly painted floral patterns and geometric designs in blue are recurrent themes for decoration in the classic Jaipur pottery. The revival in the 1960s of the Jaipur Blue pottery

Detail of a Molela façade at the Udaipur Railway Station.
Image credit: Vijay Makhija

style by Kripal Singh Shekhawat, under the patronage of Kamaladevi Chattopadhyay and Maharani Gayatri Devi, paved the way for a miniature painting approach to new decorative patterns, as well as the introduction of *deshi rang*, mineral pigments from the Rajasthani fresco tradition. Kripal Singh's legacy of the resurgence of this art form is continued in small workshops as well as larger export houses, such as Leela Bordia's Neerja International, which harness local creative expressions and visual idioms.

Pushing the boundaries of the art form with modernistic clay modelling are a few traditional potters/clay sculptors who have become contemporary artists, such as Ram Kumar Manna of Kolkata. Originally from Midnapore, Manna continued to find his "centre" in clay modelling when he shifted to Kolkata as a youngster. Untaught by art academies, Manna's impressive terracotta sculptures for both garden and indoors are based on folk myths and tales from rural Bengal. The figures have a sophistication that is the result of years of practise and expertise. His sculptures are often cast in bronze when required by clients.

The monumental Ayyanar horse and other figures are now often used as landscaping devices for a singular silhouette of public art sculptures against the horizon of the sky and clouds. Traditionally, the terracotta horses and other figurines are meant to be votive offerings to the village guardian, Ayannar. The village community offers these as a gesture of gratitude or to seek assurance for the well-being of the village and its inhabitants. These terracotta horses and figurines stand tall at the periphery of the village, ensuring protection. Palanisamy of Pudukkotai, a specialist in the making of the immense clay Ayyanar horse of Tamil Nadu, has collaborated with Pondicherry-based artists Ray Meeker and Adil Writer several times on various projects, such as large glazed Ganeshas in stoneware clay and demonstration workshops at Dakshinachitra, Chennai, resulting in the improvements of his kiln for firing. One such project was for Jaya Jaitly's exhibition *Akshara—Symbols and Scripts*, which resulted in the making of large pots incorporating Tamil text and sayings. The collaboration turned out to be a wonderful creative exercise and beneficial on both sides. Their upcoming project is to collaborate on a large 3D wall-mounted mural based on the Navagraha concept.

Neelima Hasija is an Ahmedabad-based designer who has also worked with Tamil Nadu potters to develop a range of large terracotta handmade pottery collections for the design house Rajka Designs, founded by Rajshree and Kartikeya Sarabhai. The large figurines were made with the coiling technique, which allows the maker to build large complex forms swiftly using wet clay. The design of the new collection took inspiration from and advantage of this. The collection was visualized as objects of urban utility and décor for interior and exterior residential, hospitality and office spaces. A variety of surface techniques such as engobes, sgraffito and burnishing was explored, besides

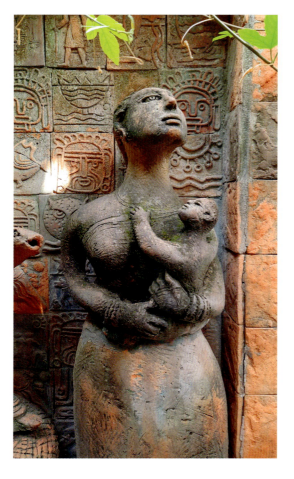

Woman and Child, life-size figure in terracotta by Ram Kumar Manna.
Image credit: Ram Kumar Manna

the traditional method of decoration, to add value to the collection.

Terracotta vessels, both large and small, are the lifeblood of the pottery craft. They supply niche forms for all functions and aspects of domestic life. Bhuvnesh Prasad comes from a pottery lineage from Rajasthan; his father, Giriraj Prasad, is a recipient of the Craft Excellence Award from the Government of India. Studying sculpture at the Delhi College of Art, Bhuvnesh has made the transition between craftsman and artist as he is famous for his large-size terracotta pots, which measure 67 x 210 inches, while his smallest miniature pot is 1 mm in height. This skilled wheel-work won him a National Award for terracotta in 2002 and a UNESCO award in 2005. Contemporary glazed stoneware pottery vessel forms are also used as multiple series in installations and space dividers within the home, for example, Vishakha Swaroop in Noida uses local terracotta as well as glazed stoneware in her works.

Dehaati Design Studio in Bhuj, Gujarat, founded by Niraj Dave, works closely with local potters such as Ramzubhai Kumbhar, Hoorbai Mamad Kumbhar and other artisans. They value traditional forms and the formulation of techniques by working on incorporating the finest of local pottery skills with a versatile range of products. They also organize pottery workshops, design facilitation tours and Kutch pottery tours. Their collaborative project in interior architecture involves making room partitions with clay toys from the village of Anjar.

The use of birds and small animals in clay is a delightful way of bringing natural forms from the exterior of the house and city into the environs of the home. Chatur Chidiyaa, a design studio founded by Rutul Shah, a design graduate from the National Institute of Design, based in Vadodara, works with the local potters' community and now runs training programmes for village adults and ITI graduates. The brand Chatur Chidiyaa started with a vision of combining the traditional skill sets of potters with meeting the current interior

and exterior décor demand. Every bird made is a true-scale replica of local birds that can be placed anywhere in the home and garden areas. The basic form is achieved through a simple clay moulding technique, with distinctive features of the bird painted in glaze on it. The combination of wooden elements with the ceramic bird adds a naturalistic minimal context to the artwork.

Kavita Pandya is the founder of Ochre Ceramics, Anand, a craft-based organization working with people from the local Rabari community and training them in the art of coloured-inlay clay—nerikomi—which is a special technique requiring immense patience and precision. The installations of local birds of Goa and other states required a tremendous amount of research for the form and characteristics of the birds as well as in the experimentation to obtain the correct colour of the clay. This requires delicate modelling of the finest of coloured clay slabs. Hanging garden mobiles inspired from marine and oceanic forms include the element of tinkling sounds as the high-fired clay slabs gently quiver in the breeze.

Terracotta roof tiles and nazar batu traditions of animals on the roofs of homes, to ward off evil spirits, inspired designer Manoj Pilli of Ahmedabad's Studio Glassic. His installation Ray of Sunshine is a response to a client, who wanted a creative intervention on the pyramidal roof of his residence away from the city. Inspired by the space itself, as well as ancient Egyptian beliefs, the image of scarabs rolling up and down the slopes, guided by the sun, was his main reference point. While he usually works with glass artisans in Purdil Nagar and Firozabad, Manoj also designs with terracotta in collaboration with Anandbhai Prajapati, who is an experienced potter from Nava Vadaj, Ahmedabad. These scarabs were sculpted in metal and terracotta clay as it is easily mouldable, has a beautiful colour and evokes a feeling of warmth and belonging. The material aesthetics subtly complemented the modern concrete building with portions of exposed brickwork. The terracotta clay was sourced from Morbi, located in the Saurashtra region

LEFT
Rekha Goyal's *Flight of the Bird*, a suspended outdoor installation in ceramic and brass for Antara Senior Living in Dehradun.
Image credit: Rekha Goyal

RIGHT
A wall and ceiling light installation by Siraj Saxena for Vana Wellness Retreat, Dehradun.
Image credit: Siraj Saxena

of Gujarat, which is the manufacturing hub of India for ceramic tiles and is famous for the production of terracotta roof tiles called *naliya*.

Ceramic mosaic is a practice that can revitalize an outdoor area by using broken or waste ceramic tile fragments in a cement base, with a coloured grout to enhance the pattern. An ancient technique, refined by the Romans on their floors and walls to illustrate myths and gods, mosaic is now a contemporary art form in the ceramic genre. Reyaz Badruddin is a ceramic artist who was introduced to the technique by Isaiah Zagar of Philadelphia about 15 years ago. Since then, he has been recycling his unwanted ceramics and mixing it with industrial tiles to create spontaneous murals. Another inspiration for him are Nek Chand's mosaic sculptures in the Rock Garden of Chandigarh and Antonio Gaudi's architectural furniture and mosaic buildings. Mosaic-like effects in glazed ceramic can also be used in ceramic logos and graphics for corporate buildings, as these are waterproof, bright and colourful and can be used to illustrate the mission and vision of the company. Shrikrishna Bhatt of Bengaluru uses a wide range of materials such as terracotta, stoneware and porcelain, along with brass, copper, steel, fibreglass and mixed media for his murals. He is well known for his ceramic nameplates that combine text, figures and decorative elements in a stunning, eye-catching combination.

Ceramics have the power to enhance mindfulness and meditative approaches in dealing with stress. The use of ceramic sculptures in wellness retreats and spas provides the ideal platform for allowing one to focus on the forms and drift away into another world. It allows the brain to relax from obsessive anxieties and soothes the stresses of contemporary life. Rekha Goyal, founder of the Pottery Lab, Mumbai, and Siraj Saxena of Delhi are two artists who have made successful installations for the Antara Senior Living and Vana Wellness Retreats in Dehradun, which merge with the ambience of the surroundings and enhance the purpose of the institution.

Ceramic objects add unique and personal touches to any environment in both the exterior and the interior. The range and versatility of the material is one of the greatest factors in its favour. The advantages of terracotta and glazed ceramic are numerous as they not only support our traditional potters by increasing the range of their creative output but are also eco-friendly, sustainable and recyclable. •

Glazed Ceramics and Terracotta

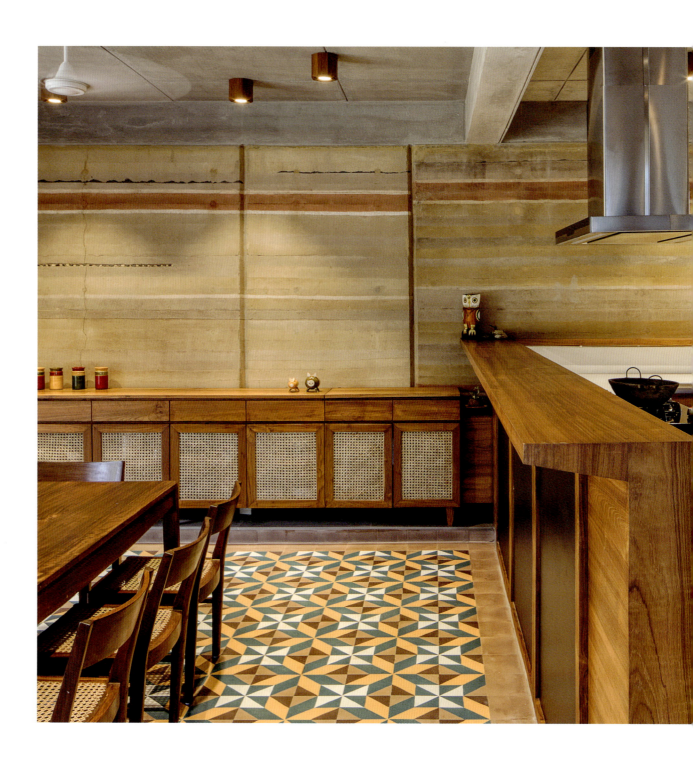

In villages, people often build their houses using mud. Bringing the same idea into mainstream architecture, we built structural walls for the house by ramming earth excavated from the site itself under the supervision of the contractor, Thumb Impression. Like patterns seen in layered sand art, different oxides were used to create layered fluid patterns in the large monolith. The earth excavated from the site was passed through a sieve and stabilized by adding binding materials. A shuttering cage was created for the walls and the earth was rammed in the middle by hand and by using metal rammers. Small pieces of rock were also used to preserve memories of what was.

Inspiration: This earth had been on the site for aeons. It had endured the test of time. And it only made sense for that earth to become the house that stood in its place.

Sustainability: The earth used is as local as it gets and so has a very low carbon footprint. It provides thermal insulation, thereby reducing energy consumption. Also, it uses only 6–8 per cent of the amount of cement usually needed for normal brick masonry. And to top it all off, it is free! ■

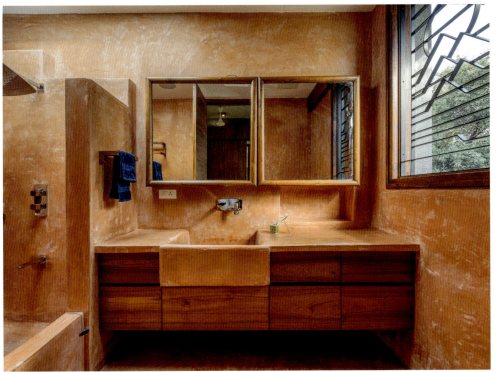

Material: Clay
Technique: Clay ramming by hand and by using metal rammers
Craftsperson(s): Bhagwanji (lime plaster), Paramjit Phull (carpentry and upcycling), Thumb Impressions (rammed-earth wall)
Source Region: Jharkhand and Chhattisgarh, India
Studio: SferaBlu, Naman Shah Architects

Glazed Ceramics and Terracotta

This mural (on the facing page), for the Grand Mercure Surya Palace Hotel in Vadodara, was monumental in size, commissioned for a rebranding of this luxury space for business travellers. For a work of this scale, primary requirements were a larger area for execution and easy access to clay and firing resources. Daroz collaborated with the small-scale ceramic industry at Thangadh, in Gujarat. Fusing the lush nature themes with highly skilled ceramic art, this mural was a way to pay homage to the cultural roots of the city of Vadodara. The works have been done in stoneware, mostly in the slip-cast and moulded techniques, with high-temperature glazes. They were fired at 1,280°C in a tunnel kiln run by natural gas.

Inspiration: There are about 225 ceramic units in the small industrial town of Thangadh, facilitating all kinds of resources and infrastructure, from professional mould-makers to tunnel kilns and highly skilled artisans. Moreover, the city is surrounded by deposits of fire clay, leading to an easy abundance of this material in the region. With this kind of access to material and infrastructure, collaborating with the industry becomes a liberating experience for an artist or designer.

Sustainability: Ceramics all start with clay, which is a naturally malleable material composed of minerals and water. They can last for centuries! Glazed ceramics are water-resistant and reduce single-use disposable products, while unglazed terracotta, which is porous and easily broken, merges back into the soil aggregate. The durability of ceramics increases based on the materials used and the temperature at which they are fired. ■

Material: Glazed ceramic
Technique: Slip-cast glazed stoneware ceramic
Source Region: Gujarat, India
Studio: P.R. Daroz

Glazed Ceramics and Terracotta • 45

Glazed Ceramics and Terracotta

The terracotta pottery of Pune has been used in interior design for two sites amidst two different functional contexts and two different design ideas. At the first site, a beauty salon, the larger idea was to create a refined space within the given site constraints. The décor, material palette and graphics were critical. Hence, rather than the more commonly used photos of models and film stars, handcrafted terracotta plates, with abstract figures of beauty, were used. At the other site, a tourism office, the underlining theme for the décor was to use line diagrams of famous tourist destinations on the terracotta plates. These plates were displayed prominently

in the visitors' area, thus influencing the spatial aesthetics in line with the theme. The process involved creating customized graphics, making the clay plates and using subtle dashes of colours or engravings to depict the ideas.

Inspiration: Terracotta work has been an ancient expression of art and culture Pune, which has survived and managed to hold its place in the modern world. The Kumbhar Wada, situated in the city's historic area of Kasba Peth, dates back to the fifth century. As a tribute to this traditional art form of Pune and to establish a subtle relation between the space being designed and the place where it belongs, it was employed in the interior design of the two locations. Eventually, these elements ended up governing the overall spatial aesthetics and became one of the focal points of the design vocabulary.

Sustainability: Bringing together innovative ideas by designers and the skills of craftsmen can widen the scope of work for those still employed in traditional crafts. The idea here was to use this ancient pottery form in a contemporary manner as an integral part of the interior space, also helping the artisan community keep a centuries-old craft alive. ∎

Material: Terracotta
Technique: Terracotta pottery
Craftsperson(s): Dhanashree Kelkar (clay artist), Tushar Kothawade and Chiranjivi Lunkad (designers)
Source Region: Maharashtra, India
Studio: Studio Infinity

Glazed Ceramics and Terracotta

Terracotta is moulded in the desired/designed form and is then fired until it turns hard. Once fired, the clay turns into a brownish orange colour, ranging from earthy ochre to red. The artwork is made in pieces and assembled on site, pasted to the desired surface using adhesives.

Inspiration: Terracotta mural works and pottery have been used since ancient times. Introducing this ancient Indian art form into contemporary interiors adds an essence of rustic beauty to the space, with its intricate details and a traditional touch of art.

Sustainability: In addition to terracotta's easy resistance to heat and climate, its longevity, strength and easy process of manufacturing make it a highly eco-sustainable material. The manufacturing process of terracotta is natural and does not include harmful chemicals. ■

Material: Clay
Craft Technique: Clay moulding and firing to create artwork
Craftsperson(s): Baaya Design, Mumbai
Source Region: West Bengal, Maharashtra, India
Studio: Manish Kumat Design Studio

Glazed Ceramics and Terracotta

Glazed Ceramics and Terracotta

This project was largely about exploring the various ways in which traditional terracotta work could be used to create products for interiors, landscape solutions and other designs. The uniqueness of this process was in blending two different types of firing in a single product: the use of oxidation and reduction in firing enabled us to obtain rich red and black colours. Also, the artisans, including many women, were encouraged to design the artworks themselves, respecting the authenticity of artisans as bearers of traditional knowledge.

Inspiration: The many challenges posed by the material and nature of the craft were the inspiration: traditional terracotta potters are among the poorest of artisans, although they possess a wealth of know-how. Furthermore, due to the depletion of local resources, the clay has to be procured across distances. Terracotta is difficult to transport owing to its fragility and hence extra care has to be taken. However, traditional pottery skills demonstrated the versatility of the craft and the adaptability of the artisans.

Sustainability: Apart from offering flexibility, clay and terracotta involve the use of natural materials throughout the process. Employing this craft also ensures that traditional skills of potters are not lost and provides a revenue stream to this community of disadvantaged but highly skilled artisans. ■

Material: Clay
Technique: Reduction and oxidation firing
Craftsperson(s): Shalini, Sundaran (mural work)
Source Region: Kerala, India
Studio: Kumbham Murals

Glazed Ceramics and Terracotta • 51

Glazed Ceramics and Terracotta

Brick is a very basic construction material, and here it has been given a twist by introducing perforations in it. A 19-mm metal framing system with pivot was created to build a kinetic screen with brick and metal, allowing for sunlight in delicate patterns and air circulation.

Inspiration: Brick is a natural material known for its cooling properties and for not transferring heat. Hence, it has been used here to provide natural light and preserve venturi effect for air circulation. It also mimics, in a contemporary way, the effect of traditional stone *jaalis*, or latticed screens, bringing a traditional art form into a modern home.

Sustainability: Bricks are essentially 100 per cent recyclable and require no maintenance. They are made from some of the earth's most abundant and natural materials, and are available locally. ■

Material: Clay, metal
Technique: Brick perforations and metal casting and framing with pivot
Source Region: Gujarat, India
Studio: Dipen Gada and Associates

Glazed Ceramics and Terracotta • 53

Glazed Ceramics and Terracotta

This building, in the peri-urban locale of Bansberia, West Bengal, was designed to serve the local community. Collaborating with a ceramic artist, rejected ceramic blocks (originally procured for industrial use) were collected. Terracotta bricks were procured from a riverside brick field located nearby. These two were combined, using locally prevalent finesse of building masonry, to give a vibrant contemporary expression to an ancient building form of Bengal.

Inspiration: Based on a decision to introduce another architectural idiom to the community, the building took cues from Bengal's terracotta temples, which have a long history in the region. Exposed brick masonry walls, inlaid with ceramic blocks, define the character of this

building as a contemporary expression of the inspiration.

Sustainability: Industrial waste, in the form of rejected ceramic blocks, was used along with locally sourced terracotta for this project. This ensured that the project had a very low carbon footprint, in addition to continuing an age-old building tradition. ■

Material: Custom-made paints
Technique: Traditional masonry
Craftsperson(s): Partha Dasgupta
Source Region: West Bengal, India
Studio: Abin Design Studio

Glazed Ceramics and Terracotta • 55

Glazed Ceramics and Terracotta

The natural clay paste, formed of organic materials, was used on the wall surfaces to create a pleasant, appetite-stimulating aroma. Reclaimed jute was used to create some of the furniture elements and some partition screens, as well as the ceiling for acoustic purposes. The paintings on the surfaces were done by the client's family of potters, creating a stronger connection with the space and their family heritage. The utensils and serving dishes were also made of clay, reinforcing the traditional values and connection to nature.

Inspiration: The main source of inspiration was the craft heritage of the client's family, who were in the tradition of pottery and terracotta work. Moreover, budget constraints and a respect for the environment made clay and reclaimed jute an ideal choice for this space. The weaving of vernacular and modern technology, and the collaboration and contribution of the local stakeholders in the family and the architects, has resulted in spontaneity and diversity in the design.

Sustainability: This project has a carbon footprint of zero, largely because the designers followed the philosophy of biophilia, which is strengthened by using clay in its various expressions. All the materials used are organic and naturally derived, and the design team took pride in the fact that no artificial binding agents or dyes were used. Furthermore, the involvement of the client's family in the design DNA of this space ensured a deep connection and a spatial narrative that is rich and will endure for generations. ■

Material: Clay, natural dye, turmeric, grain husk and binding agent, reclaimed jute
Technique: Traditional pottery, jute weaving
Craftsperson(s): Pappubhai, Bhupendrabhai
Source Region: Gujarat, India
Studio: The Grid Architects

Glazed Ceramics and Terracotta

Traditional building crafts play an essential role in the design of interior spaces. For this residence, the designers wanted to bring in the essence of the homeowners' South Indian heritage in a modern residence. As one enters the hallway to the living room, the visitor is greeted by an explosion of ochre, with bright multi-coloured Athangudi tiles used for the flooring. Making the tiles involves first fixing a transparent glass piece to a metal frame to achieve the right size. After the pattern is selected, a stencil is used to pour different coloured mixes in a sequence or, alternatively, a freehand design is created. This mixture is then layered with a dry powder of sand and cement and overlaid with mortar. Following this, the tile is dried and cured. The glass plate offers a smooth, non-slippery finish, and can be embossed or engraved for textural variety.

Inspiration: The inspiration for using these tiles comes from their traditional use in palatial mansions of the Chettiars. The tiles, still manufactured by hand, can be customized into any geometric pattern, or floral or any other motifs, and size and shape, as per requirement, which offers an added advantage. Each tile is made individually, with the slight imperfections adding a sense of novelty to the craft. The use of Athangudi tiles helped add a 'wow' factor to the space and give a traditional South Indian look to a modern residence in north India.

Sustainability: Athangudi tiles are very eco-friendly due to the use of local materials and no burning of fuel. These cement tiles use the locally available sand, natural oxide colouring and water in a traditional handmade fashion. Though many new production methodologies are available with technology innovation, Athangudi tiles are a prime example of preserving an age-old traditional practice while still adapting them in modern times. Moreover, they tend to get shinier with use and are 100 per cent maintenance-free. Since these are still made by hand, they do not use any energy-consuming mechanisms and are biodegradable. ■

Material: Ceramics, sand, cement, synthetic oxides
Technique: Athangudi tiles
Source Region: Tamil Nadu, India
Studio: Envisage Projects

Glazed Ceramics and Terracotta • 59

Glazed Ceramics and Terracotta

Hailing from a lineage of traditional potters, B.R. Pandit and his sons Abhay and Shailesh executed one of their largest art commissions, on the concept of the element of water, for installations at the Mumbai international airport. The artwork starts with 1,100 ceramic *shivling*s depicting water hung on the ceiling like a galaxy, with a mirror image on the ground. The water body is seen in the form of clouds on the background of glazed ceramic walls and pillars. One can touch the flow of water coming out of the stone spouts, which create a musical sound like that produced by a *jal tarang*.

The approximate size of this installation is 60 feet in length, 20 feet in height and 18 feet in depth, with a weight of approximately 24 tons. All the work was handmade at their studio using lots of textures, high relief work and deep carving with a stoneware clay body, with copper oxide and barium carbonate glazes. All the pieces were high-fired in a gas kiln in an oxidation atmosphere.

Inspiration: Panditji's journey from Bhadrawati to Mumbai and the setting up of a studio pottery-style workshop showed a new direction for the combination of hereditary and vernacular skills with contemporary sensibilities. This fresh visual language is lushly demonstrated in these artworks, which fuse ceramic art with the esoteric concept of the element of water from the *panchamahabhuta*, the five physical elements crucial to life in the universe.

Sustainability: Both terracotta and high-fired glazed stoneware clay are useful for clay modelling and textured surfaces. Stoneware is durable and waterproof while terracotta, being porous, requires protection from direct rain. ■

Material: Glazed ceramic and terracotta
Technique: Handbuilt and moulded, glazed stoneware ceramic and terracotta
Source Region: Maharashtra, India
Studio: Brahmdeo Ram and Abhay Pandit, Mumbai

Glazed Ceramics and Terracotta

This outdoor installation was designed to cool the air naturally, based on the properties of terracotta pots, or *matka*s. The finished product is viewed as a piece of functional art, where it is cocreated with experienced craftspeople from potters' communities in Delhi, Uttar Pradesh and Bhuj. While the CoolAnt team provides the design, it is the hands of the experienced potters that craft and bake the terracotta pots. These are then combined with a metal framework, made by a fabricator, and other components which allow the water to trickle down and the hot air passing through the pots to get cooled.

Inspiration: Traditionally, in many parts of India, terracotta pots or *matka*s have been used to keep water cool during summers. Inspired by this property of the material along with form exploration to naturally cool air, our products use terracotta pots arranged like a beehive to reduce the temperature of both water and air. As a result, we are able to provide passive cooling and create thermal comfort in both indoor and outdoor spaces.

Sustainability: The design of the terracotta cones maximizes the surface area and the evaporative cooling effect, in addition to channelizing airflow. The material is sourced locally, and hence, in terms of embodied energy and impact on the environment, its carbon footprint is much lower than plastic or metal. The installation is inspired by passive cooling techniques and uses very low energy for cooling in built spaces.

Material: Terracotta, metal framework
Technique: The moulding of terracotta pots for natural cooling
Source Region: Uttar Pradesh, Gujarat and Delhi, India
Studio: Ant Studio

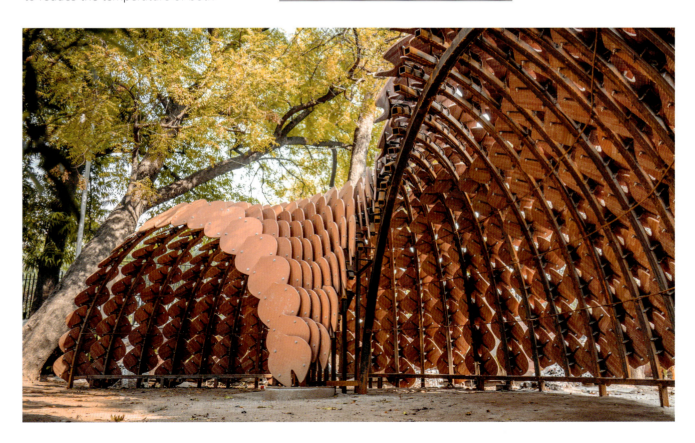

Glazed Ceramics and Terracotta

Clay slabs, fired terracotta, high-fired ceramics and black-and-white *raku* pieces were used in various ways in this project. Clay slabs, made locally in Lalpur, Gujarat, were used here as surface decoration; the flame marks on terracotta give the interior space a very mystic quality that goes with the feminine that is celebrated in space design. Brass hooks, called *patu*, which hold these dry-clad terracotta slabs, were used to give the design the richness and shine of metal, to complement the earthen natural feel of fired earth.

Inspiration: The simplicity and versatility of Indian crafts aligned very well with the brand value of this handloom and textile brand, which provided us with an opportunity to experiment with traditional craft for the interior and exterior design of this space. Moreover, accepting the maxim that change is an inevitable part of life, the designs were conceived as fully recyclable, in case of any future changes or reuse of the same.

Sustainability: Most of the materials were locally sourced from regions in Gujarat and Puducherry, where the client is located. Given the low environmental impact of using traditional crafts and methods, the potential for reuse is very high. There is also a strong element of social sustainability, which helps to reskill many craftspeople and provides employment to them. ■

Material: Ceramics
Technique: High-firing ceramics, *raku* pottery
Craftsperson(s): Bhupatbhai/Dhrafa Studio, Karan Kumar/Tharam Ceramics, through Rakhee Kane/Aavartan, Auroville
Source Region: Gujarat and Puducherry, India
Studio: Dustudio

Glazed Ceramics and Terracotta

Ceramic arts are an age-old tradition native to many parts of the world. In this project, this tradition has been used to create a screen, which acts as a partition between the dining space and the prayer area, or *puja* room. The screen is made of stoneware clay and glazed and fired at 1,200 °C. A "form-work" is given to the artisan to give them a precise size to work with. The final production and assembly begins after taking into account the shrinkage post-firing. Each individual piece of the screen is unique and handmade, which contrasts with the uniformity of an industrially made product.

Inspiration: Ceramics is a popular medium owing to the wide availability of the material. It has its own distinct nature and type according to its source region. Its handmade, customizable nature, which varies from one artisan to the other, gives it a great deal of charm and warmth.

Sustainability: Ceramics is essentially clay, a material found in geological abundance and with a shelf life of millennia. Artefacts of clay made in ancient civilizations are still being recovered today, many intact, demonstrating the timelessness of this material. Its presence throughout human history has allowed it to adapt with the times, making it always relevant to contemporary needs. Although much revival work has been done, we have only explored the tip of the iceberg in the use of ceramics in architecture and interiors. ■

Material: Stoneware clay
Technique: Glazing and firing stoneware clay
Source Region: Maharashtra, India
Studio: Reasoning Instincts Architecture Studio (RIAS) with Industhan Ceramics

GRASS, COIR AND NATURAL FIBRES

Embracing the Planet

• Neelam Chhiber

Importance of Natural Fibres in Our Daily Lives

Natural fibres have been with us since the dawn of mankind. Flax, for example, is said to have been used for burial shrouds since the time of Egyptian pharaohs. Irrespective of geography, fibres of native plants are being utilized to make a wide variety of products, from apparel to building materials such as cordage, roofing, structures and walls, and energy through biomass. Even the automotive industry sees their value in car body interiors.

Following the present state of ecological imbalance, there has been a growing concern over the detrimental effects of synthetic fibres and their impact on our health and environment. Natural fibres, if utilized properly, can be a massive boost to the economy of developing countries. Hence, the sectors involving natural fibres look at a future that is not only beneficial to our environment but can also address social and economic sustainability.

Primarily, natural fibres such as bamboo, jute, flax, hemp, sisal, agave, coir, seagrass, river grass and banana are considered to fall under the "hard natural fibres" segment. They can easily and efficiently replace synthetic, non-renewable materials such as glass, ceramic, aramid and boron, which are not only expensive but also add to the carbon footprint in production. Other advantages of natural fibres, in addition to being eco-friendly and low-cost, are that they are found in abundance, have low density and high cellulosic mass, and are biodegradable and non-abrasive to processing. Upon incineration, natural fibres also leave considerably less residue as compared to

synthetic fibres. In the last century, all natural fibres have come under tremendous pressure due to the production of man-made fibres and synthetic alternatives. Now, we see an upswing due to deep climate change concerns and scientifically proven data, showing the adverse impact of excessive chemicals in home and work environments on the human body. Additionally, natural fibres usually have specific characteristics with regards to end use, and cannot be easily substituted.

Experience of Working with Natural Fibres

The Kumaraguru College of Engineering, in Coimbatore, has introduced state-of-the-art infrastructure and facilities in their labs for spinning and weaving, under the Kepak Board as its centre of excellence. Looking at the abundant availability of bananas in India and the scope it has for extracting fibres and producing excellent items, the project was formulated to use the fibres in the area of textiles. The processes involved procuring banana fibres, softening them with enzymes, spinning them into yarns, weaving them into fabrics and making articles of utility out of those fabrics. The project involved a three-way spinning system. The first is the jute-spinning system that obtained the fabric from banana yarn, jute and banana blend and used it for interior furnishing and window blinds. The second procedure, called adhesive splicing, produced fibres that made *kurtas*, table linen and shopping bags as an alternative to plastic bags. In the third procedure, hand knotting is woven into decorative *pallus* for saris. Among these, the most common is jute-spinning, but the yarn count is too low. In certain cases, bananas are often spun with cotton or silk

PREVIOUS PAGES
Jute ropes provide a way to manipulate sunlight and air in this rooftop cafe.
Image credit: The Grid Architects

Women weave screw pine in Tamil Nadu.
Image credit: Mapin

using open-ended spinning. To make the yarn suitable for weaving and comfortable enough for wearing, adhesive splicing is used to unite filaments and provide a twist to the yarn.

The processing of natural fibres is usually tedious and labour intensive, which demands justified value at price. Hence, the product is viable in international markets, bringing revenue for the country.

Industree, working with artisans across villages in India, noted that urbanization is growing unsustainably, due to the dearth of employment opportunities in villages in spite of the presence of treasures in raw material and related traditional skills. The organization's mandate was to look at the means to scale up, so that the stake of Indian artisans in national and global markets could increase and they could earn more. Industree Foundation has worked with Government of India schemes and mobilized artisans into self-help groups. Those working with banana bark are members of Green Kraft Producer Company, a cooperative of more than 2,000 women. Green Kraft was initially seeded by the Office of Development Commissioner (Handicrafts), followed by many national and international donors. In addition, Industree Foundation has a history of working entirely with lesser-known natural fibres, such as river grass, sisal, palm leaf, palm *naar*, palm stem, *shital pati*, elephant grass and water hyacinth, etc. It provides these groups with access to markets, designs and finances, improved raw material supply, improved technology and value engineering. Under the Babasaheb Ambedkar Hast Shilpa Vikas Yojana, the Foundation has also introduced design and skill-building programmes to train 7,500 women in 28 districts, across seven states of India.

The team of Kadam works with *sabai* grass, bamboo and smaller fibres in the districts of West Bengal. They conduct workshops on these materials and collaborate with different craft groups to make products for everyday use. *Sabai* grass, another abundantly found natural fibre in our country, plays an important role in generating economic value for the tribal population of our country.

Villages in the district of Mayur Ganj, which has a solid percentage of tribal population below the poverty line, depend on the primary sector, as *sabai* grass is the only agricultural product marketed there. *Sabai* grass leaves are long and produce high-quality fibre, so they are mostly used in the manufacturing of paper, but being flexible and strong, they are also used to make ropes and rope-based items. The processing of *sabai* grass involves cutting, drying, repeated boiling, washing and finally drying in the sun. The grass is then dyed, plaited and twisted into ropes and then developed into baskets using different techniques.

Crafts Practised with Grass, Coir and Natural Fibres Across the Country
From Kashmir to Kanyakumari, Guwahati to Gandhinagar, India has a rich history of handicrafts carried on for centuries. Each region has its own essence, and the crafts belonging

there reflect its uniqueness, geographically and culturally. While there are innumerable crafts and traditions throughout the country, the ones made of natural fibres should be specially mentioned.

Natural fibre crafts are generally produced where the raw materials are found in abundance, away from the cities. However, nowadays, these crafts catch the eyes of urban customers who, gradually shifting towards ecological awareness, are greatly impressed by the versatility of natural fibres and their ability to replace plastic products.

Coir

A natural fibre made from the husk of coconut, coir is commonly known as coconut fibre. It is used in making floor mats, doormats, brushes, brooms and even mattresses. The fibrous material found between the hard, internal shell and the outer shell of the coconut is extracted to make coir. Another variety, called white coir, found in unripe coconuts, is used to make delicate items such as strings, ropes and fishing nets. The structure of the coir fibre is such that it can absorb and retain moisture, making it strong and flexible.

Coir products have a wide application range in embankment protection, slope protection and rural road development. Coir becomes an excellent replacement for wood products as it can be easily used to build composite boards for furniture and infrastructure (recorded to have been used in building relief homes). Newer innovative uses of coir include mats for wall panelling and compressed discs of coir as tabletops.

The technicalities in processing coconut husks involve two methods—coir retting and mechanical processes that are further subdivided into defibering and decorticating processes, the latter used in reducing the length of the fibre.

The Coir Board has now standardized the various coir products and by-products, such as coir-pith, which has recently been found useful in agriculture and horticulture. To promote

A woman weaves a *madur* mat as a wedding gift for her younger brother, in West Bengal.
Image credit: Mapin

small-scale industries in the country, the Coir Board has developed schemes in which critical types of subsidies are provided to coir industries. The Khadi Board has also provided a scheme under which up to Rs 15 lakhs worth of subsidy is given for any unit of coir.

Khus

Khus (*Vetiveria zizaniodes*), also called *ramachan* in Malayalam, is an aromatic root of densely tufted grass. Its thick root system is extremely helpful for checking soil erosion and strengthening banks. Found mainly in the states of Rajasthan, Uttar Pradesh, Punjab, Kerala, Karnataka, Tamil Nadu and Andhra Pradesh, it is used for making mats, beds, thatches and pads for desert coolers, especially due to its cooling properties. High in utilization, it is also used for making a refreshing summer drink, whilst its stem is used for making blinds.

Grass and Reed Fibres

Mostly used in making crafts and regular products, grass and reed fibres are referred to in local regional languages as *moonj*, *sarkanda*, *korai*, *sikki*, *chipkiang*, *madur kathi*, rice straw and *kauna* reed. As reeds grow naturally in marshy land and in ponds, they are widely available and used in several different ways.

- *Kauna:* The sight of women weaving mats, square and rectangular cushions and mattresses from the cylindrical, soft and spongy stem of *kauna* (family *Cyperaceae*) is common in the Meitei community of the Imphal Valley in Manipur. The raw material for the craft is obtained by simple processing, wherein the reed is cut near the base of the plant and dried in the sun. In order to preserve and store it for a longer time, it is often smoked. The mats have interwoven and interlaced stalks of jute threads, made with simple tools, and have the ends finished uniquely by hand. *Kauna* mattresses and cushions make excellent furniture items and have great scope in modern furniture and interiors.

- *Korai:* Known as *korai* (Tamil Nadu) or *kora* (Kerala), also of the *Cyperaceae* family, this grass is another wetland plant cultivated in Tamil Nadu. The stems are cut, spliced and dried in the sun. When the dried stems turn into a smooth and tubular form, a large variety of mats are made with stripes and geometrical motifs using natural and dyed colours. The mats are woven on horizontal floor looms. The ribbed natural-coloured mats are popularly used as floor coverings in houses. Here, again, the potential is enormous, right from shaping the finer mats into upholstery to furniture and interiors, such as blinds, floor cushions and wall cladding.

- *Madur Kathi:* Madur (*Cyperus corymbosus*) is another type of reed, similar to *kora*, found in Midnapur, in West Bengal. Found in every Bengali household, finely spliced *madur* is woven into mats that have a central field enclosed by patterned borders. The weavers ingeniously use two subtly differentiated naturally coloured splits, or selectively dyed parts of the splits, to create unique geometrical patterns, with the borders woven tightly so as to not allow breakage. Though the weaving technique is quite simple, it requires traditionally learned craftsmanship. These mats are great for all kinds of interior décor.

- *Murta:* The *murta* plant (*Maranta dichotoma*), is used to make *shital pati*s, woven mats that have a naturally cooling effect. Harvested when green, *murta* stems are washed in soda water and dried. Then they are boiled and sliced into strips for plaiting, giving the mat a smooth and lustrous texture. Growing around water bodies in Cooch Behar, West Bengal, *shital pati*s and *nakshi pati*s are manufactured mostly in Assam and Tripura.

- *Moonj:* Women make baskets in Uttar Pradesh and Bihar using the technique of coiling. These are made for local use with spliced *moonj* or *sikki* grass stalks. The trays and shallow containers are used to store food grains and flour. *Moonj* baskets with multi-coloured fibres and bold patterns are traditionally made for a daughter's trousseau.

Grass, Coir and Natural Fibres • 69

LEFT AND RIGHT
A variety of stylish products, made with traditional craft techniques, for modern living, by the Industree–IKEA partnership.
Image credit: Inter IKEA Systems

- *Sikki:* In the Madhubani region of Bihar, women make figurines of deities, animals and birds for ritual and everyday use with *sikki*, or golden grass, used in combination with multi-coloured dyed stalks. The imagery of these forms echoes the folk art of Mithila, the cultural region on the northern banks of the Ganges.

- *Sarkanda:* A wild grass found in Haryana, its long stems are used in making the indigenous *mooda*.

Palmyra Palm
Strips from palm leaves are used to make coiled baskets and containers in Tamil Nadu and Haryana. A bunch of grass fibres forms the core material of the coil, and a palm leaf strip is wound over the coil and binds consecutive rows of coils in place. Palm is one of the most versatile natural fibres in the world, with different parts of the leaf having different properties. The fibre of the frond arm, which attaches it to the tree, is used for the production of the bristles used in shoe brushes and traditional shaving brushes, among other products. The palm leaf frond itself offers two or three types of fibres, used in different kinds of basket making.

Date Palm
Strips from date palm leaves are used to make coiled baskets and containers in Haryana.

Pandanas Palm (also known as Screw Pine)
This is a tropical plant grown as a hedge or as a boundary wall in Kerala. The utilization of screw pine provides a source of income to rural women who make strips from the leaves to weave mats. The leaves are also used as roof thatches. Strips are interlaced diagonally to weave mats and large surfaces, which are then cut and sewn to make containers, bags and hats. The female species of the screw pine produces a finer quality of fibre, used in weaving traditional mats, called *mettha pai*, which are soft and cool and used as bedding. The male screw pine has a coarser fibre with rugged edges. In Thazava, a small town in Kollam, Kerala, double-layered mats are made with edges of vividly coloured strips. The mats are also burnished with a stone that gives them a polished sheen.

Jute
A stem or bast fibre, jute is found extensively in West Bengal. Jute cloth is brittle and deteriorates with exposure to sun and rain, but it has gained immense popularity as an

inexpensive packaging material. Nowadays, there is a renewed interest in finding innovative applications of jute, such as fashion accessories, bags and wall panelling, using macramé, crochet, braiding and other non-woven techniques in the craft and creative manufacturing sectors.

Natural Fibres in Interiors

Initially used to make gunny bags to store rice, pulses and so on, jute has increasingly gained appeal as a sustainable fabric that acquires forms such as home utility items, décor pieces, lamps and chandeliers.

Coir, from the land of coconut trees, forms the base of an industry that employs millions of men and women, who produce beautifully crafted products for daily use and decoration such as ropes, baskets, floor coverings, doormats, lamps and scrubbers. Durable across all seasons and geographies, coir is a hot favourite for interior designers for unique, sustainable and eco-friendly decorations.

The advantages of using natural fibres are that these are a safer option for flooring and furnishings in the family home, as well as being more breathable, thermo-regulating and helping to cleanse and purify the air indoors.

As the world is dumped with plastic, more than it can manage, baskets make an aesthetically pleasing alternative to plastic storage boxes in the living room, side counters, kitchen pantries and cupboards. Sturdy baskets made

of reed, grass and other fibres also make a great alternative to plastic pots for indoor plants. Fibre-cloth materials make excellent covers for soft furnishings, bedding, curtains and even clothing for a more eco-conscious individual.

Sisal fibres, which are used to make cords and strings, are nowadays used for carpeting, as well as strongly promoted in automotive interiors, in the shaped moulding of the interiors of car bodies. Using natural fibres in our homes and offices gives us a cool, bohemian and cosy atmosphere without having to step out. Not only is it aesthetically pleasing, it is also good for the pockets and the environment, while at the same time giving a chance to preserve and protect the rich tradition of craft carried on for centuries before us.

Conclusion

Developing the natural fibre sector and facilitating its way to our daily living is a means to not only develop and promote alternatives to synthetics and timber that would help protect the planet's ecology, but also address the issues of socio-economic development, poverty and exclusion. Time and again, natural fibres have emerged as a sector that is deeply embedded with empowerment, equity and economic development of marginalized communities. The products, when put on a worldwide market sphere, boost rural economies and also help retain a cultural heritage and aesthetic taste that India has nurtured for centuries. •

Grass, Coir and Natural Fibres

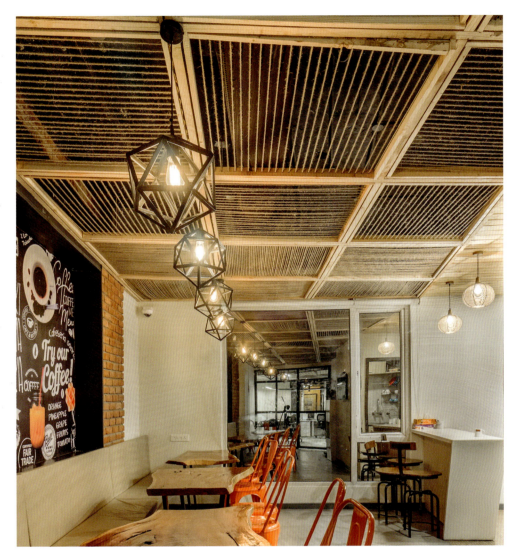

This project involved the design of an office set up by an international firm, which wanted an office with an Indian touch. We found fibre ropes quite promising and developed ideas to utilize this craft innovatively for the project based on the sustainable approach of "Recycle—Reuse—Reduce." This not only led to employment opportunities but also helped in the revival of the age-old *charpai* weaving tradition in a more relevant and modern way. Skilled artisans from an East Delhi village were hired to weave the fibre panels in ceilings. Different weave patterns were explored to define the formal and the informal areas within the office space. We worked in close coordination at the site with the weavers to develop terminating and overlapping details.

Inspiration: Fibre ropes are a material widely available throughout the country and used in a variety of interior and exterior applications. Here, fibre ropes established the project's concept of frugality and transparency. The product has good elasticity and is a useful material for sound absorption. The rope patterns helped us achieve interesting ceiling designs and at the same time accentuated the space.

Sustainability: Fibre rope is a material with a high recycle value. The material is indigenous to the region and hence has a low carbon footprint. Also, it can be easily reused within any other space. ■

Material: Natural fibres
Technique: *Charpai* weaving
Source Region: Delhi, India
Studio: Studio CoDe

Grass, Coir and Natural Fibres

This project featured a close-to-nature palette, with jute ropes, recycled wood, sunlight and other such materials. The rope canopy gave the space direction, sharpness and sophistication. In addition to these, the weave of the ropes made sure to liberally harness sunlight, which is abundant in Ahmedabad. Moreover, watered jute can also help keep the surroundings cool, which is a valuable attribute in the hot, dry climate of the city. The flooring was recycled babul wood, sourced at a very low cost and in an eco-friendly manner from the forest department. All the materials were worked on by local craftspeople.

Inspiration: Since building by-laws precluded any permanent or semi-permanent structure, the humble Indian *charpoy* became the main source of inspiration. The *charpoy* structure defined individual seating islands, hanging lamps and canopies. This allowed for an earthy look and the modulation of light and shadow in a very enchanting manner.

Sustainability: The material palette here is dominated by recycled materials, such as jute rope, babul wood, gum, corrugated sheets and MS, aluminium and stone. The other major "material" was sunlight, which is abundant and free. Jute is very eco-friendly and when watered, it can help cool the surroundings. All materials were locally sourced following the philosophy of bio-philic design. ■

Material: Jute
Technique: Weaving jute ropes
Craftsperson(s): Pappubhai, Bhupendrabhai
Source Region: Gujarat, India
Studio: The Grid Architects

Grass, Coir and Natural Fibres • 75

Grass, Coir and Natural Fibres

Trilegal's new offices form the canvas for a series of vibrant Indian art and craft forms, executed in collaboration with artisans commissioned by Dastkari Haat Samiti. The underlying design idea was to capture diverse craft forms found in the country to create distinct spatial identities for each zone. *Sanjhi* paper stencilling, which has origins in the temples of Mathura and Vrindavan, was reinterpreted in a contemporary format to showcase Delhi's architectural landmarks and rich biodiversity. The fixture creates a backdrop for the reception, separating it from a conference room in the office. The intricate paper cuts have been sandwiched between glass panels to reinforce their integrity and are scaled up to form a backdrop to the reception. Conventionally used white paper has been replaced with a black one to screen the meeting room from direct view.

Inspiration: Ram Soni is a renowned *sanjhi* artist who makes elaborately patterned artworks and large panels out of paper as a departure from ritualistic expressions for temples in Vrindavan. He needs only a pair of scissors as his tool. For this project, his *sanjhi* craft was chosen to depict the historic buildings and landmarks of Delhi, in addition to its diverse flora and fauna, combining the charm of forests and excellence in architecture.

Sustainability: The *sanjhi* craft requires only sheets of paper and a pair of specially designed scissors to develop the intricate cuts and patterns used to create the designs. Its simple nature requires no mechanical intervention, and thus it has virtually zero environmental impact. ■

Materials: Paper, scissors
Technique: *Sanjhi* paper cutting or paper stencilling
Craftsperson(s): Ram Soni (*sanjhi*), Dastkari Haat Samiti (graphics)
Source Region: Uttar Pradesh, India
Studio: Studio Lotus in partnership with Dastkari Haat Samiti, New Delhi

Grass, Coir and Natural Fibres • 77

BAMBOO, CANE AND WILLOW

Fresh Breezes Stir Bamboo and Cane

BAMBOO, CANE AND WILLOW

Fresh Breezes Stir Bamboo and Cane

• Rebecca Reubens

Bamboo and rattan furniture and décor elements have been part of material culture and interior design in India since ancient times. Bamboo's versatility and ease of use allow the bamboo-working communities to use this material from the cradle to the grave: an infant's umbilical cord is severed at the time of birth with a sharp bamboo blade; and the people are carried to their last rites on a bamboo stretcher. Through their lifetime, bamboo is integral to their different activities. They eat and cook in bamboo, live in bamboo houses and use bamboo for fuel, furniture and daily utilitarian items, as well as implements for agriculture. Rattan, known colloquially as "cane," is another ancient material that has been used extensively by indigenous communities to build structures, ranging from small artefacts to the homes they live in, and even bridges that help them establish connectivity with the outside world.

In contrast to the crafts of working bamboo and rattan, which have existed as indigenous crafts of India since time immemorial, the crafting of willow baskets was introduced to Kashmir from Europe in the 19th century by Maharaja Hari Singh. In the early 20th century, the principal of Kashmir's first technical institute, an Englishman named Mr Andrews, introduced English willow as a raw material in and around the marshes of Bage-Dilawar Khan and began to teach wicker weaving at the institute. Since then, willow reeds have become an integral part of the Kashmiri *kangri*—a small clay pot held in willow basketry—which holds live coal embers and is worn under clothing, literally close to the heart, as a small personal heater during the cold Kashmiri winters. Several "English-style" products still prevail, a legacy of Mr Andrews's technical centre. Over time, willow has been

woven into contemporary and commercial items, from baskets to carry Eid gifts in, to dustbins, laundry baskets and lighting.

While bamboo, cane and wicker are referred to by different scientific and local names by different craft communities, in mainstream interior design, all three materials are often commonly called "cane" or "wicker." This shared ubiquitous term seems to imply that these are the same or similar; however, all three materials are distinctly different in terms of their morphology, properties and applications. Bamboo is a giant woody grass, which has around 1,500 species and populates most parts of the world. Rattan, on the other hand, is a vine from the palm family, which has around 600 species, and is primarily found in Asia and Africa. Willow is a deciduous tree or a shrub, which has around 400 species, and is generally found in high-altitude regions in the northern hemisphere. Structurally, these materials are almost antithetical. Bamboo is a rigid, generally hollow tube with discs inside it at the "knot," while rattan is a flexible, solid rod. Willow is a solid rod in broad-ranging sizes, whose bark, or "withy," is peeled off before it is used. Perhaps one of the reasons these three materials with almost opposite structures and properties are referred to interchangeably is that they can all be woven into mats and three-dimensional structures, sometimes by converting them into smaller sections called "slivers." Another reason for the misinformation around the materials could be the same as that which plagues most craft materials: they are not part of mainstream design education and, therefore, designers are not fluent with their properties, applications and production-to-consumption systems.

PREVIOUS PAGES
A craftsperson spends a pleasant afternoon weaving a basket.
Image credit: iStock

Various members of a family engage in the making of *kangri*s in Chirar-e-Sharif, Kashmir.
Image credit: Mapin

A woven bamboo chair and bamboo side-table featuring a vintage *tagara* designed by Studio Rhizome for an interior project with Errol Reubens Associates for Rann Riders Dasada.
Image credit: Studio Rhizome

Until recently, most mainstream designers have seen "wicker" furniture and décor as a low-cost, low-quality option for outdoor spaces, such as patios and gardens. However, neither bamboo nor rattan or willow is ideally suited to exterior applications, because, in their natural form, they are susceptible to weather, insects and fungus. Unsurprisingly then, "cane" furniture placed outdoors ages rapidly and ungracefully, contributing to the perception that these materials make for low-quality interior elements and therefore should be low-cost as well.

The perception that bamboo, rattan and willow furniture is "cheap" is reinforced by the fact that a large volume of "cane" furniture is indeed badly designed and poorly finished. Most of these pieces are sourced from small contractors or craftspeople churning out "modern" products for tourists on the sides of highways or in tiny shanties. These products are produced by craftspeople desperately looking to extend their market avenues because their traditional market systems are collapsing. This urgent need exists because, post-industrialization, craft-based production-to-consumption systems—and the craftspeople integral to them—have been jeopardized by the influx of nationally and internationally produced industrial products, which have captured their market segment; plastic has replaced baskets made from these materials, and also rattan webbing. Simultaneously, the physical and virtual connectivity of the industrial and information revolutions has exposed consumers—including rural buyers—to globalized lifestyles, to which they now aspire. This preference for technology over tradition, and for mass-produced substitutes over craft products, has disrupted traditional localized production-to-consumption systems, resulting in a loss of livelihoods for craftspeople—thereby contributing to poverty and unemployment.

This untenable situation is compounded by the tragedy of the commons. Bamboo and rattan craftspeople no longer have free access to the forests they historically accessed as common property. The Indian Forest Act of 1865 vested ownership of forests and common pastures with the state, making forest-dependent communities—including bamboo and rattan craftspeople—trespassers in the forests from where their ancestors gathered the input materials for their craft. Worse still, these communities cannot turn to agriculture since they do not own land. With a lack of any other productive skill except for their craft, no land to farm, no access to their raw material, and shrinking markets, most bamboo and rattan craftspeople are in dire need of livelihood. Fortunately, willow is available relatively easily,

Bamboo incorporated as drawer and door handles, lighting installation and curtain rods at the Kamala Foundation's store at Gandhi Ashram in Ahmedabad, by Studio Rhizome and Errol Reubens Associates.
Image credit: Studio Rhizome

especially in the semi-marsh lands north of Anchar Lake and the vast areas of Ganderbal. However, like the bamboo and cane craftspeople —and indeed most craftspeople in India— identifying new markets is imperative for their survival and the sustainability of their craft.

Interestingly, the same industrial and information revolutions that jeopardized traditional markets now offer lucrative new patrons in the growing and emerging markets for sustainable products and lifestyle options. Sustainable design has become non-negotiable against the backdrop of the environmental damage caused by unprecedented industrialization and development. One rule of thumb that has emerged is to use renewable materials, which grow on the surface of the earth, instead of non-renewable materials, which need to be mined and take millions of years to be regenerated. Given that almost three-fourths of the materials we use post-industrialization—such as coal, natural gas and oil—come from below the surface of the earth, the spotlight is on renewable materials from the biosphere, including bamboo and rattan. Bamboo is of special relevance against the backdrop of the sustainability crisis as it is one of the fastest-growing renewable resources known to man; some of the faster-growing bamboo species can grow up to 30 inches in a day!

Materials such as bamboo, rattan and willow can address both environmental sustainability (as they are renewable) and social sustainability (as they can potentially be crafted by traditional communities and restore and create livelihoods).

Juxtaposed against the backdrop of the sustainability crises and the consequent burgeoning sustainability market, these seem like materials positioned to serendipitously connect the dots and create a win-win situation. Unfortunately, this opportunity is not realized because designers nowadays veer away from craft products (which they perceive to be old-fashioned and of low value) and towards industrially processed versions of these sustainable materials (which they perceive to be cutting-edge and of high value).

These industrially processed materials emerged in the Global North, where the focus on sustainability has historically been eco-centric. These materials are made from reconstituted bamboo, which is held together with glue that is generally quite unsustainable. The resulting materials—including bamboo composites, bamboo plywood, bamboo veneer, bamboo-oriented strand boards, corrugated bamboo mat-boards—position industrially processed bamboo as a fast-growing substitute for hardwood. This positioning has been lapped up by the interior design fraternity, who have applied these materials in numerous design projects, which have received positive media attention. These design-led, industrially processed, technology-push bamboo products have demonstrated that, through design, non-mainstream renewable materials can find commercial viability in sustainability-aligned markets. However, recent studies have questioned the ecological sustainability of these products, given their huge carbon footprint when they are exported or transported over large distances. In addition to perhaps not being as ecologically sustainable as first imagined, these products have also failed to leverage the materials' potential to contribute to social and cultural sustainability by addressing issues of poverty and livelihoods. This is because industrial products do not translate into livelihoods for indigent producers in traditional craft clusters, where a substantial percentage of production takes place. These communities lack the financial capital to invest in the technology that is required to manufacture these product lines. Therefore, they go from being involved in and benefitting from every node of non-industrial value chains, to having limited involvement in industrial value chains—mostly in growing, managing, harvesting, transporting and processing bamboo at the most primary levels.

This scenario has focused global attention on the fact that design efforts, even if aligned to sustainability markets and involving green materials, need to go beyond green design and commercial viability if they are to impact sustainability—including its ecological, social, cultural and economic dimensions—in a balanced and holistic manner.

Serendipitously, traditional craft seems to hold points of departure for holistic sustainability through design. Traditional craft has always used renewable resources from the biosphere—including bamboo, rattan and wicker—due to their easy availability in the natural environment. The products that result are incredibly refined and nuanced and have evolved and been perfected over a significant period of time with tremendous bio-regional sensitivity and cultural significance. The communities in the north-east of India, especially, have achieved astounding and poetic feats of

Detail of flattened bamboo wall in Tripura.
Image credit: Rebecca Reubens

Kotwalia craftsperson shows the large bamboo basket she has crafted in Dang, Gujarat.
Image credit: Rebecca Reubens

architecture and design, ranging from rattan bridges to bamboo fishing baskets. Rattan and bamboo are materials of choice in these regions, owing to their easy availability in the natural environment, their versatility and their being easy to process with simple tools. Unlike wood, which begs for tools and machines to process it because of its radial grains, bamboo's vertical fibres make it easy to process using very basic tools: in most cases, traditional bamboo-working communities craft a wide repertoire of incredibly detailed and complex products using a sickle-shaped knife, called *dao*. Cane and willow are also processed relatively simply, using simple handheld tools and local resources.

The stark contrast between the refinement of traditional bamboo, cane and wicker products and the low-cost and low-value products produced by the same craftspeople for non-traditional markets is intriguing. One reason for this phenomenon is the craftsperson's inability to visualize what urban markets want. Designers can bring value to this process as collaborators in the innovation process. The collaboration between designer and craftsperson maximizes the skill and knowledge that each brings to the innovation process. The craftsperson brings indigenous knowledge and practices that have been validated over time as sustainable. Many of the concepts of sustainability have underpinned craft practice, such as the use of local materials or expertise, and production in a single material, which allows for ease in sourcing, production and repair, and also in eventual disassembly and recycling. The designer brings value with their access to information and technology on current issues, including sustainability. Both inputs are complementary and supplementary.

Emerging collaborations between craft and design have been heartening and have resulted in beautiful, unique and bespoke interior spaces. This is a testament to the fact that the synergy between craft and design can free bamboo, cane and willow craftspeople from the burden of the hand and heart needing to impersonate machines—of producing cookie-cutter products with a machine-made ethos, which are deeply antithetical to the idea and character of the handcrafted. Remarkable examples of Indian interiors reveal that it is indeed possible for bamboo, cane and willow craft to inhabit and be essential parts of contemporary interiors in a manner that is relevant, valued, affordable, and therefore ideally placed to impact sustainability for all of the factions involved—craft, design and the world.

The hope is that the inspiring work in this vein will proves that the boundaries between craft and design are porous and that indigenous producers need not be indigent. The incredible beauty of vernacular interiors using bamboo, rattan and willow can, in some part, be transferred to contemporary Indian interiors to create spaces with poetry and soul. •

Bamboo, Cane and Willow

We deconstructed traditional craft into elements and then transferred them into our interior design in different scales. We created a cladding on the main façade with bamboo culms. The internal windows are all fitted with bamboo screens. Bamboo tubes were used for lighting, and cabinet and door handles were all created by handcrafting bamboo using the traditional skill-set. The process began with selecting the correct bamboo age and species for each element. The bamboo was further worked on by hand, by splitting it using a *dao* and heat-bending it using a flame where required. Burning was also used in some places to add colour to the bamboo and treat it. Finally, the bamboo was sanded and polished by hand.

Inspiration: Bamboo is widely available across the country and is an extremely versatile material, both in terms of techniques and scale. This is the reason our studio works primarily with bamboo and traditional bamboo-working communities in Tripura and Gujarat.

Sustainability: Bamboo is one of the fastest-growing plant species, regenerating quicker than other trees by giving out new shoots every year. It is a carbon sink, controls soil erosion, purifies water and rehabilitates land, and doesn't depend on irrigation. It helps marginalized communities economically and is easy to process using minimum equipment. ■

Material: Bamboo
Technique: Splitting, heat-bending, burning
Source Region: Tripura and Gujarat, India
Studio: Errol Reubens Associates

Bamboo, Cane and Willow • 87

Bamboo, Cane and Willow

For this project, the objective was to use the materials not as add-ons but as part of a seamless experience. Mud was stabilized and finished with lime wash. Bamboo was treated for longevity and finished with external-grade PU coat, and the furniture joints were bound with cane for strength and aesthetics.

Inspiration: The five elements—Earth, Air, Fire (Sun), Water and Space—were the main inspiration for the design and construction of spaces for peace and harmony in this project. The idea was to make the ambience of the house dissolve in the background without obstructing, as is the case with most of our traditional spaces.

Sustainability: Mud and bamboo are among the most sustainable materials to be used in buildings and interiors. Bamboo is a highly resource-efficient material due to its rapid growth and is extremely versatile in usage. Moreover, its use also supports vulnerable bamboo-based communities, thereby conforming to the three Ps—People, Planet and Profit. ∎

Material: Bamboo
Technique: Traditional processing and construction
Craftsperson(s): Gopal Kr Tanti, Syed, Uttam and Anandilal Marandi
Source Region: Karnataka, India
Studio: Manasaram Architects

Bamboo, Cane and Willow

Wicker is made from plant-originated material—willow, rattan and bamboo—and is widely available across the country. In our projects, the "skeleton and skin" structure methodology is followed, with the internal parts being made of lightweight rattan or powder-coated M.S. frame, while the external part is woven with natural rattan.

Inspiration: We were always smitten by the colourful baskets displayed by the roadside by *banjara* groups in Hyderabad. While working with complex geometry, we once sat down with the same weavers to explore our piece "Imli" and were surprised to discover a product that was seamless in construction and exhibited rattan in its unadulterated colour and textures. Handwoven rattan has fluidic properties when applied to moulds. Additionally, the manufacturing system makes the products extremely light, making large-scale interior applications an achievable goal.

Sustainability: The manufacturing process employed here is energy-efficient and resource-efficient, making it a zero-waste technology. In addition, these are renewable and fast-growing materials, available in most parts of the country, which makes them easy to procure. All the raw materials used in these designs are biodegradable and made from renewable sources. ■

Material: Cane
Technique: Weaving
Source Region: Southern and north-eastern India
Studio: The Wicker Story

Bamboo, Cane and Willow

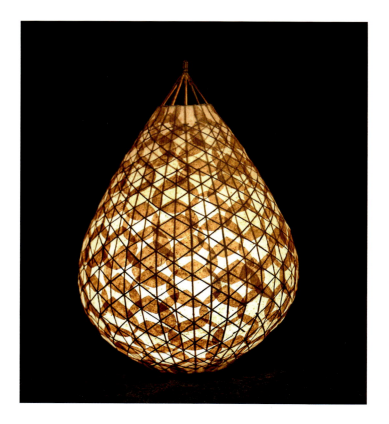

*Tazia*s are cultural symbols from the procession of Muharram. This project reinterprets this practice to create innovative design solutions such as décor, lighting and art installations. The bamboo stem is finely sliced into thin bendable sticks out of which the framework of the product is prepared. The outer skin of the frame is banana-leaf paper, assembled in a geometric pattern topped with water-resistant finishes to amplify functionality.

Inspiration: The huge and intricate structures of *tazia*, made of bamboo, have never been looked at from the lens of craft before. The technique is so versatile that most kinds of organic and geometric forms can be created just by bending the bamboo material. The final products are lightweight, durable and eco-friendly.

Sustainability: Bamboo is natural, abundant, renewable and sustainable, with a low carbon footprint. ■

Material: Bamboo, banana-leaf paper
Technique: *Tazia* making
Craftsperson(s): Azimuddin
Source Region: Rajasthan, India
Studio: AnanTaya, AKFD

Bamboo, Cane and Willow • 93

Bamboo, Cane and Willow

Truss-Me features a collection of bamboo products which embody the design philosophy of Sangaru Design Studio. Developed in close association with traditional bamboo workers and craftsmen, this collection explores a new construction technique using bamboo poles and splits, creating modular forms for a variety of new applications. Truss-Me uses bamboo's inherent property of high tensile strength and its various mechanical properties to create a structure system that is light, strong and formally pleasing. The laminated modules act like a truss—a lightweight, load-bearing frame structure.

Inspiration: Truss-Me was developed in close collaboration with the traditional artisan community that understands this material the best. With traditional practices and knowledge fast disappearing, we are constantly working with native artisans to bring about a change in the way craft is perceived. All the bamboo artisans, originally from Tripura, work full-time at Sangaru. Their know-how of the material, combined with Sangaru's design philosophy, provides the basic inspiration for these works.

Sustainability: Bamboo is a fast-growing material, which can be naturally replenished. Moreover, providing the traditional bamboo artisans a way to utilize their skills in new ways creates employment and social sustainability. ■

Material: Bamboo
Technique: Creation of bamboo modules using poles and splits
Source Region: Tripura, India
Studio: Sangaru Design Studio

Bamboo, Cane and Willow

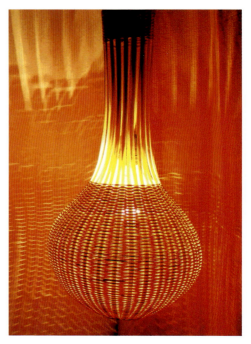

Bamboo is possibly the most commonly occurring plant in Tripura. It is prominently used in the construction of houses, fences, agricultural implements, mats and basket weaving. The bamboo craft of Tripura is acknowledged for its finely made splits, artistic weaving and construction. This pendant lamp is a remarkable example of bamboo basketry. The traditional basketry technique used to make mats has been used here with ingenuity to become a ceiling-mounted pendant lamp. Long splits span the entire length of the lamp, interwoven at the base, creating a complex geometry through which speckled light spills out.

Inspiration: Made by the traditional bamboo artisans of Tripura, basketry of the lamp was done in a manner that made the structure of the bamboo splits evident, and this strongly built lamp appears deceptively delicate. Light passes beautifully along the length of the splits and creates a speckled effect. Fibreglass, which is toxic as well as ecologically disastrous, is widely used to create moulds for baskets. Here, it has been replaced by shaping the basket on a terracotta pot made by a local potter in the desired shape.

Sustainability: Bamboo is a regenerative plant and grows to its usual height within four years. Staggered harvesting allows craftspeople and farmers to grow this easily. Utilized by tribal as well as non-tribal communities of the state in various practices, its use has no negative impact on ecology and does not contribute to deforestation. When the basket is finished, the pot is broken and goes back to the earth. By linking the making of the lamp to a local potter, the process creates an inter-dependent livelihood. ■

Material: Bamboo
Technique: Bamboo basketry shaped on a terracotta pot
Craftsperson(s): Artisans from the Tripura Bamboo Mission
Source Region: Tripura, India
Studio: Siddhartha Das Studio, New Delhi

Bamboo, Cane and Willow

The Trojan Seater is built by attaching thick heat-bent cane rings to a 32-inch truck tyre core. Rope made from waste fabric is then used to create a weave pattern over this structure. Traditional basketry techniques from the east and north-east of India are adapted, with the breadth of the tyre allowing for a range of intricate pattern interactions. Finally, a single metal ring is attached to the base to create classic hairpin legs that create an illusion of weightlessness. Discarded tyres are sourced from large auto-dealers. Rope is made from waste generated by the sari and denim industries and purchased from units in Ahmedabad.

Inspiration: Using the expanse of a truck tyre as a canvas, the seater harnesses the interplay of a rubber frame and a flexible weave structure to create a piece with both strength and give. The seater draws from distinct pattern languages—from *phulkari* to houndstooth textile patterning.

Sustainability: This design utilizes truck tyres, particularly radial tyres, which cannot be deconstructed or reused because of their composition. Additionally, it uses waste rope made from scraps from the sari industry and yarn from the resource-heavy denim manufacturing process. These materials, instead of being discarded, are recognized for their unique aesthetic features and their longevity. ■

Material: Automotive tyres, cane, fabric-waste rope
Technique: Traditional basketry, textile weaving, heat-bent cane frame
Craftsperson(s): Siraj Ansari
Source Region: Punjab, Gujarat, Assam and Karnataka, India
Studio: The Retyrement Plan

WOOD

New Roots for Old Trees

WOOD

New Roots for Old Trees

• A. Balasubramaniam

Wood is the most versatile material known to mankind. It is also among the oldest known natural resources. If you are looking for a material that is adaptable to geometric shapes and organic forms, amenable to hand tools and power tools, where size is not a constraint and scale is not a barrier, then wood is your material of choice.

A piece of wood has a unique look and feel, almost like a fingerprint, that bears the legacy of the tree it came from. India is blessed with an abundance of raw material that has resulted in every state developing a unique craft in wood. The kind and quality of wood differ from state to state: walnut, teak, *sheesham*, mango, rosewood, pine and sandalwood are just some of the notable ones. Ancient Indian architecture is replete with examples of houses, temples and palaces with exemplary use of wood. The royalty in Kashmir are said to have engaged artisans to decorate their houses and palaces with intricate motifs from nature. The hill houses of Himachal Pradesh show a unique building technique called *kathkuni*, in which wood and stone are held together without mortar, enabling the buildings to survive earthquakes. Whether it is the *haveli*s of Gujarat or the temples and palaces of Kerala, wood has been a favoured material for building and construction for centuries and across climatic conditions; from cold, snowy places to hot, tropical ones, wood has been the chosen material for exterior elements or interior spaces.

India has some outstanding examples of wood craftsmanship in household products as well. Wood products can be embellished by carving, turning, inlaying, lacquering, painting and other processes. All of these have different colours, weight and workability, giving each craft a distinct design language. The colourful

PREVIOUS PAGES
A detail of the installation at the Ministry of External Affairs, in New Delhi, featuring stone and wood carving and papier-mâché.
Image credit: Jatin Bhatt

*Haveli*s such as these were built primarily with wood, and had huge courtyards. The entire house would be a frame structure in wood. The wooden lintels and the lacing in the walls were not mere décor, but earthquake-resistant construction techniques prevalent in this region.
Photo Credit: Deval "Pino" Shah/
www.ArtByPino.com

toys of Channapatna, turned out of local varieties of wood and finished to perfection with lacquer on manual lathes are examples of this. With the distinctly carved chests of Saharanpur, inlaid with elegant brass wire; the eagle thrones with tribal carvings, found at the Nagaland *morung*s; and the minimalistic and colourful turned-wood furniture of Gujarat's Sankheda, we have a unique range of crafts and techniques that are adaptable for modern use.

Artisans use wood for products that are so unique that they are impossible to replicate. The carvings on a jewellery box made of walnut wood, the brass inlay on a teak photo frame or the delicate wiry forms of sandalwood carving—these designs are worked upon by master craftsmen, making each one remarkably different. This gives the artisan an edge over mass-produced products, as such work is impossible to be executed by machines.

The library of motifs, techniques, patterns and forms has been handed down and honed through generations of artisans to perfection. The artisans carry in their heads a huge collection of forms and shapes, ready for use in making products that are delightfully diverse. There is a growing need to document this collective knowledge so that they are protected from exploitation.

The ease with which artisans work with wood is a sight to behold. Artisans are now experimenting with new forms and adapting to modern techniques of making to find new clientele for their wares. Design interventions have helped develop new products, repurpose old ones and create custom-made, contemporary designs that cater to refreshingly new markets. There is a growing interest among architects and designers to keep these crafts alive, and they are keen to expand their vocabulary and create new opportunities for the crafts. This leads to a novel range of products that are new expressions of old and classic patterns, forms and techniques. Lamps, photo frames, mirror frames, trinket boxes and small items of furniture have been transformed from looking plain and mundane to elaborate and enticing by using crafts. Design has been responsible for these innovative products, giving crafts a new lease of life.

Working with artisans to design and make new kinds of products is an act of co-creation. Designers find fresh opportunities for the use and adaptation of artisanal skills, while the artisans themselves possess a repertoire of patterns, finishes and techniques that is humbling. Together, this symbiotic partnership lends itself to the creation of exciting interiors and products. Designers may get new ideas as they learn from traditional artisans the strengths and limitations of the craft and material, and artisans understand designing and making for a context. Not only do designers learn to apply crafts as embellishments on furniture and interior products, but they also contribute to making production easier by shifting basic processes like cutting, sizing and finishing to machines, enabling a quicker turnaround time.

Sankheda *hichako*.
The quintessential *hichako*, found in almost every Gujarati household in different forms, is a popular product of Sankheda craft.

Wood • 101

A carved and painted embellishment to the roof of a temple in Payyanur, in Kerala.
Image credit: Dastkari Haat Samiti

BELOW
The nail-free, modular joinery craft that adorns ceilings of homes and houseboats is one of the prized skills of Kashmir.
Image credit: Dastkari Haat Samiti

A temple in Chamba, Himachal Pradesh is made of carved wood on the exterior and interiors as well. Image credit: Dastkari Haat Samiti

Designers are always making a choice between their love for trees and their love for wood. It may come as a surprise to many that wood is a very sustainable material, as it is a renewable resource and has a low carbon impact. The energy required to produce artisanal products in wood by craftsmen is negligible as most of the processes are manual, compared to those of mechanical production. Most artisans procure wood from sustainable and regulated resources, which makes it an ideal material for use in the contemporary context.

Imagine an intricately carved Kashmiri wooden screen, in the place of a fibreglass partition, which can bring excitement to an office. Get dazzled by living rooms with colourful Sankheda furniture that becomes a conversation starter. Be intrigued by the brightly painted wooden closet doors that resemble a *kaavad* in a bedroom. Add pizzazz to a child's nursery by adorning it with a turned-wood lamp made and finished like Channapatna turned-wood toys! The contemporary expressions of India's timeless wood crafts are limited only by the imagination of the designer.

The win-win partnership between the designer and the artisan leads to the imaginative adoption of wood in contemporary interiors, making them most sought after by artisans, architects and designers. Wood, which has fuelled our homes and hearths for centuries in the past, will now fuel the revolutions of designed interiors and products for centuries to come. •

Wood

Kaavad is a 500-year-old unique Rajasthani tradition of crafting stories on a wooden box. Designed as a portable shrine to mythological Hindu deities or local saints, it has multiple wooden panels hinged together and painted with visual narratives. In a traditional *kaavad*, the shutters are painted red and the partition frames yellow. For this project, the *kaavad* was used as inspiration for creating a full-size cupboard for the owner's extensive collection of saris.

Inspiration: The idea of the storytelling box was applied to the owner's "sari library," which opened in multiple ways, inspired by the traditional *kaavad*. Instead of a mythical folk tale, it tells the story of the owner—"Priya *ki kahaani*"—and her quest across India to discover various

textile traditions. The painted visuals, each on a different wooden panel, begin in a sari shop and continue across Varanasi, Puri, Bengal and Kutch, eventually ending the tale showing her sari cupboard.

Sustainability: This *kaavad* cupboard was designed and executed by traditional *kaavad* artists, and the visual narratives were painted by the artist Dwarikaji Prasad Jehangir from Chittorgarh in Rajasthan. Hence, there is a strong element of social sustainability, which helps keep centuries-old traditions alive. ■

Material: Wood
Craft technique: Hand-painting on wood inspired by a traditional *kaavad*
Craftsperson(s): Dwarikaji Prasad Jehangir
Source region: Rajasthan, India
Studio: S+PS Architects

Wood

Two hundred wooden modules were crafted and used as a ceiling installation at a sushi and dim sum parlour. Large 900 mm beams that dissect the space were clad with mirrors on four sides, thereby reflecting the installation and creating an illusion of infinity. The deliberate contemporary forms and modern colour schemes bring the local Channapatna craft into an unexpected spatial context, that of a vibrant, trendy East Asian restaurant.

Inspiration: Channapatna is located near Bengaluru, and we wanted to work with artisans in a township that was local. The wood offered numerous possibilities, both in terms of form and colour options that worked well with the restaurant concept.

Sustainability: Locally sourced hale wood and FSC-certified wood from industrial surplus waste has been used along with reclaimed teak. All dyes are

Material: Wood
Technique: Channapatna woodworking (lathe turning and lacquer-dyeing)
Craftsperson(s): Syed Mubarak, Salimbhai
Source Region: Karnataka, India
Studio: MAIA Design Studio in collaboration with Atul Johri

natural (sourced from Himalayan regions) with natural shellac (sourced from East India). The production processes are aligned with the goals set up by the United Nations Sustainable Development Group for creating sustainable livelihood opportunities for rural craftspersons and artisans. ■

Wood

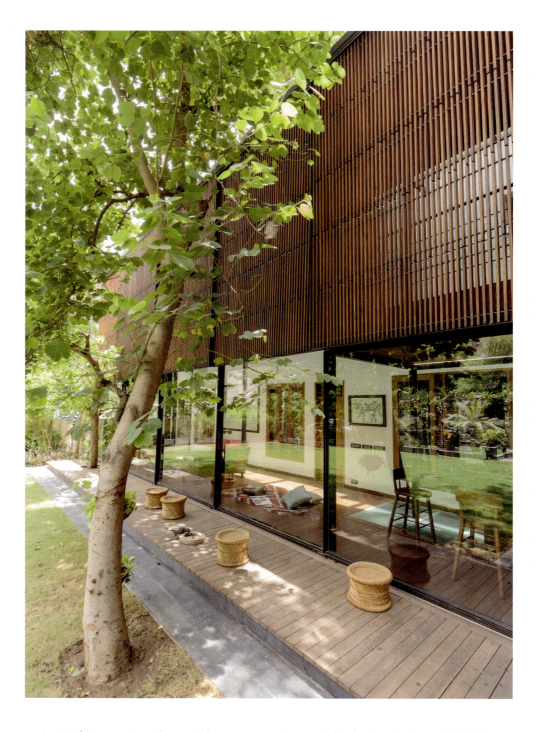

Wood is an extremely versatile material, available across the country in a variety of species with different characteristics and qualities. *Shou sugi ban* is an old Japanese technique of wood preservation, in which the surface of the wood is treated through a controlled fire, making it resistant to water, rot and pests without the need for further treatment. In this project, this technique was taught to and quickly adopted by local craftsmen.

Inspiration: With wood, the possibilities are endless. For the project with the wooden slats, sliding panels with teak battens were flexibly deployed to shade the space and maintain privacy, while still

letting in light and air. For the Black Perch project, the charred, treated wooden louvres were used to give a distinctive look to the house while still keeping it linked to the old house it was added to (as a homage to the old *pol* houses of Ahmedabad city, which had dark wooden façades).

Sustainability: Wood is locally available and the Japanese *shou sugi ban* technique protects the wood from water, rot and pests. Overall, this increases the durability of wood and minimizes the need for further protective interventions. ■

Material: Wood
Technique: *Shou sugi ban*, a Japanese technique of wood preservation
Source Region: Gujarat, India
Studio: Studio Sangath

Wood

The production process starts with the material selection, the wood being locally sourced teak. Experienced carpenters then produce the raw handcrafted furniture item. The entire woodcarving process is carried out by hand using traditional carpentry tools. The unpolished carved wooden furniture pieces are passed on to the varnishing workshop, where they are sanded and sealed.

Inspiration: Wood and cane complement each other really well. Since the 15th century, Europeans living in the subcontinent replaced fabrics and upholstery with cane as it lasts beautifully in the hot and humid climate and it is native to the area. These pieces of furniture reflect the best creative collaboration between the East and West by combining traditional Indian craftsmanship with European designs to create a new vocabulary of luxury.

Sustainability: Natural wood is gaining popularity once again for use in furniture, with responsibly sourced and reclaimed wood being particularly favoured. A reused piece of wood is a great way to lower the carbon footprint. ■

Material: Wood, cane
Technique: *Marapani* (wood carving), weaving
Source Region: Kerala, India
Studio: Temple Town by Meera Pyarelal

Wood • 111

Wood

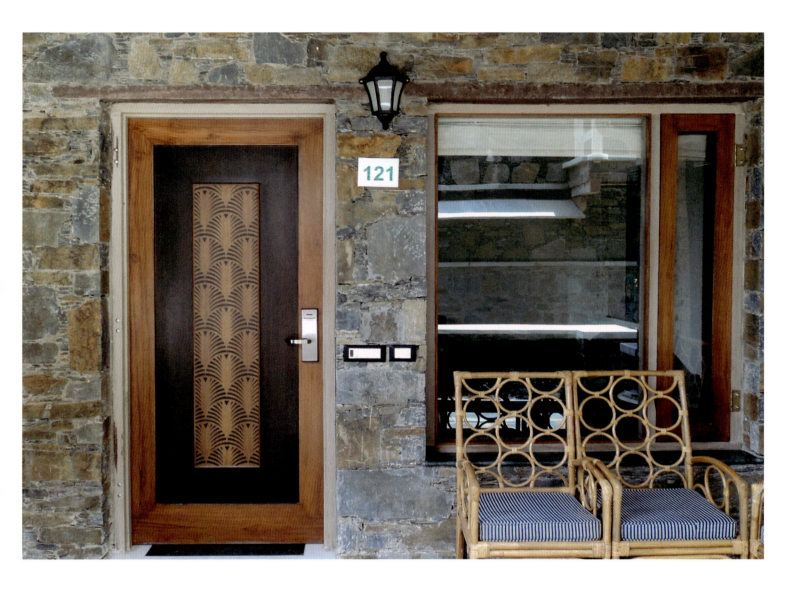

Inlay is a closely protected traditional art. This delicate process involves carefully engraving and inserting pieces of coloured materials into depressions in a base object by hand. To begin with, a predefined pattern or design is engraved on a base material. After this, pieces of the same material in a contrasting colour, or a completely different material, are cut precisely to fit into these grooves. This is done in a way that the inlaid material is flush with the base. Such inlay work adorns contemporary interior spaces with a traditional stroke. For example, in Ramada by Wyndham Resort, Udaipur, the wood-in-wood inlay on the door of the peacock-themed room has been inspired by peacocks, while the ivory acrylic inlay door has been inspired by the solar lineage of the ruling family dynasty of Mewar.

Inspiration: The inlay work is inspired by various palaces and *haveli*s of Rajasthan that feature artworks deeply rooted in the architectural style of Mewar. This traditional artwork has been beautifully modernized to create fascinating and innovative furnishing surfaces in a combination of materials.

Sustainability: Adaptation of such crafts in contemporary designs helps in employment generation for the traditional craftspersons who are the bearers of the wealth of our traditional knowledge. The material used for the craft is natural and timeless, and does not require extensive use of machines, making the designing process less polluting to the environment. ■

Material: Wood, veneer, acrylic
Technique: Inlay
Craftsperson(s): Narayan Chauhan
Source Region: Rajasthan, India
Studio: Abhikram Architects, Panika Crafts, and Technologies

Wood

Being abundantly available in Kerala, timber is synonymous with the state's traditional style of architecture. The timber used for this particular project has been exclusively sourced from Kallai, famed for having the highest quality, and then seasoned for durability. The craftsmanship showcased in the woodwork is what essentially forms the key feature of this design. The intricate detailing has been hand-carved by expert "*ashari*s," who come from a traditional lineage of carpenters.

Inspiration: Traditional woodwork in Kerala was typically executed in timber, which is abundant in the state. This has also given rise to an exceptionally talented pool of carpenters and woodworkers who can execute a wide variety of designs. Hence, it was decided that using carved timber would not only be sustainable and versatile, but its naturalistic features would also help create a design narrative that complements the landscape.

Sustainability: All the wood used here was locally sourced from Kerala and a new sapling was planted for every tree that was cut in order to ensure that the natural plant ecosystem was not disrupted. Moreover, timber offers a high potential for reuse, thereby reducing waste after construction. Being a material that possesses low thermal conductivity, wood is an ideal and sustainable choice for humid climates in places such as Kerala. ■

Material: Wood
Technique: Traditional wood carving
Craftsperson(s): Ashokan
Source Region: Kerala, India
Studio: BCA Architecture

Wood

The design of this main door is inspired by the traditional decorative arched doors commonly found in Rajasthani architecture. The "carving" on the door was achieved by CNC routing into several layers of birch ply. The frame and inner openable shutter were made using traditional joinery and the curved brass pull handle was bent to shape by a metalworker.

Inspiration: Birch ply was chosen over regular ply as it has a void-free core, which displays beautifully straight lines on the carved and chamfered edges. The use of mirrors is reminiscent of the *meenakari/shisha* work found in Rajasthani architectural and textile/jewellery design. Overall, the design was meant to bring the essence of Rajasthan into a modern, contemporary home.

Sustainability: Birch trees are abundant and a fast-growing species, and the birch ply is made from FSC timber. ■

Material: Wood
Technique: Wood carving, traditional joinery
Craftsperson(s): Bhagwan Suthar (carpentry and polish work) Pritesh Shah (CNC cutting), Ratna Gupta (artwork)
Source Region: Maharashtra, India
Studio: Studio Hinge

Wood • 117

Wood

Nine installations were created on the theme of "flora" for the premises of the Ministry of External Affairs (MEA) in New Delhi. The ceremonial lobby installations shown here featured *dhokra*, or lost-wax casting, from Bastar; walnut-wood carving and papier-mâché from Kashmir; stone carving from Rajasthan; wood carving from Gujarat; and brass and copper embossing from Uttar Pradesh. The artisans were sourced from various regions of crafts practice.

Inspiration: The core idea was to demonstrate the various possibilities embedded within the theme of "flora" as a composite visual expression, using as many different Indian craft forms as possible. The artworks in the ceremonial lobby at the MEA premises are a celebration of living Indian crafts, visible to all visiting dignitaries, guests and employees of MEA, with all formal welcoming functions for diplomatic exchange held in this space.

Sustainability: Crafts, by virtue of their handmade nature, are inherently sustainable, as they support creative cultural industries and livelihoods of the practitioners as an antidote against mass production and consumption. Many crafts such as *dhokra* metalwork and steel forging in Bastar use scrap metals as raw material, thereby allowing for the reuse of waste. The other crafts also use locally sourced material and employ age-old methods of craftsmanship, ensuring the survival of these skills. ■

Material: Papier-mâché, wood, brass, copper, stone, fabric, steel
Technique: *Dhokra* metal casting, wood carving, papier-mâché, stone carving, metal embossing
Craftsperson(s): Gangaram (brass embossing), Manzoor and Rasheed (walnut woodcarving), Fayaz Jan (papier mâchè painting), Rajaram (stone carving), Santhuram, Nirmal and Sundar (dhokra metal casting and forging) and Malay (wood carving)
Source Region: Uttar Pradesh, Kashmir, Rajasthan, Chhattisgarh and Gujarat, India
Studio: Jatin Bhatt

Wood

"Upcycling" art is a technique that requires many hours of exploring and experimenting with the materials and their possibilities, as well as time to collect the waste. This ingenious method allows for immense potential, as wood waste generated and discarded during construction and other processes can be reused in meaningful and beautiful ways.

Inspiration: Artist Santanu Dey has carefully collected wood waste that was discarded during construction and the making of furniture. He used these pieces to create this amazing artwork. Unlike concrete, the rate of recycling of wood is very low; it is hoped that projects like these will demonstrate the versatility and potential embedded in the upcycling of wood.

Sustainability: Waste wood is the second-largest waste component of construction and demolition (C&D) debris after concrete. It contributes to as much as 20 to 30 per cent of a building's total C&D. It also accounts for as much as 10 per cent of the waste that is dumped into landfills. The environmental benefits of recycled art include its contribution to the use and extension of the life of materials and, as a consequence, reduction in the amount of waste generated. ■

Material: Waste wood
Technique: Upcycling waste wood
Craftsperson(s): Santanu Dey
Source Region: New Delhi, India
Studio: Somaya and Kalappa Consultants

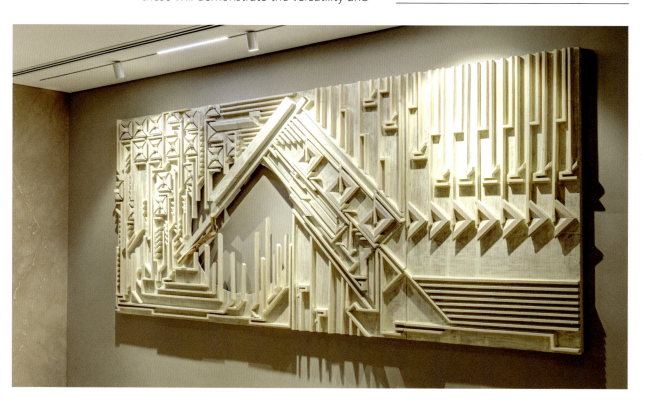

Wood

The traditional process of lacquer work on wood was repurposed here for larger wooden elements. Age-old wood-turning techniques were used to create handcrafted teak wood furniture. The lacquer was then applied in bright colours while using the wood-turning technique, after which the wood was polished and the product was assembled.

Inspiration: The aim was to showcase the versatility of lacquer work in a contemporary design. Since this technique is mostly used on small toys, it was adapted to larger pieces of furniture while retaining the bright colours and patterns to give it a vivid appeal. The result evokes the joy and nostalgia of childhood, drawing on both the memory of similarly painted toys and the vibrant colours.

Sustainability: This product used refurbished teak wood. Also, the craft of lacquer work was given a fresh boost with this new application, generating skills and employment for traditional artisans. ■

Material: Wood
Technique: Lacquer work
Craftsperson(s): Anilbhai Suthar (lacquer work), Ketanbhai and Lalitbhai (wood-turning), Ishwarbhai and Deepakbhai (carpentry)
Source Region: Gujarat, India
Studio: Thisandthat

Wood • 121

Wood

Wood carving is indigenously found in most parts of India. These projects were for a hotel in Himachal Pradesh and a sari shop in Bengaluru. For the former, the hotel corridors were decorated with wood carving styles local to the area, using locally available wood. The sari shop in Bengaluru featured carved wooden panels depicting floral motifs and other designs from Andhra Pradesh.

Inspiration: Himachal Pradesh has many temples that feature beautiful woodwork. This inspired the designs in the hotel corridor, with local craftspeople and local materials. For the sari shop, inspiration was taken from the designs on the sari borders, predominantly floral motifs. Hence, the same was carved on the wooden panels.

Sustainability: For both projects, local materials were used (deodar and white oak), and local craftspeople were trained as carpenters and polishers to execute the designs. Wood, if treated well, can last very long and will remain pest- and climate-resistant. Moreover, it can be upcycled and reused for other products, reducing the carbon footprint. ■

Material: Wood
Technique: Traditional wood carving
Craftsperson(s): Sri Kalahasti (wood carving), Aditi Prakash/Pure Ghee Designs (wood carving), Windmill Furniture (shaft detail)
Source Region: Himachal Pradesh and Andhra Pradesh, India
Studio: Pradeep Sachdeva Design Associates

Wood

Chamba *rumaal* embroidery applies the *do rookha* technique, which lends it a distinctive character by making this embroidery reversible. In order to best showcase the dual-sided embroidery, the textile panels have been integrated into a wooden structure made from salvaged wood with dark polish to create a contrast for the base fabric (pure unbleached natural silk) of the embroidery panels.

Inspiration: This space divider-cum-storage unit highlights the reversible nature of the traditional craft of Chamba *rumaal* embroidery. The design depicts the journey of this intricate technique from mere threads to a story crafted onto fabric, where the textile panel is accompanied by the elements that go into its creation, thus reinforcing the essence of the craft. What was once a textile piece has now been incorporated in a new avatar as multi-functional furniture.

Sustainability: The space divider was built using reclaimed wood and wood composites, thus reducing the carbon footprint by reusing/recycling materials. Using silk in its pure, natural form is another way of ensuring minimal damage to the environment. The finished product also revives a dying craft and can generate economic benefits for traditional practitioners of this craft. ■

Material: *Do rookha* embroidery, woodwork
Technique: Chamba *rumaal* embroidery, woodwork
Craftsperson(s): Lalita Vakil
Source Region: Himachal Pradesh and New Delhi, India
Studio: Pearl Academy—Interior Design Department
Aishwarya Maini, Anushka Tiwari and Mamta Agarwal (students)
Puja Anand, Urmimala Bora (faculty)

TEXTILES

Flow of Fabric Enters a New World

TEXTILES

Flow of Fabric Enters a New World

• Jaya Jaitly

India's romance with its own textiles is deeply ingrained in the psyche of its people—an unselfconscious, internally embraced, outer-skin kind of experience. Whether it is a young girl in the village who has a sari draped on her by her mother for the first time, or a bride who revels in the gold and silken fabric that embraces her on her wedding day, it is an intrinsic part of the life of its people. Fabrics flow gracefully off the handloom, or are embellished by women who create embroidered decorations on them to tell stories, bless their daughters with coverlets or quilts on their wedding day, or express the identity of their community and the region of its origin and cultural history. Political histories, too, have influenced the production of cloth for different classes of people in society, and international movements have further guided the production of specific kinds of textiles in India over

centuries. Indian textiles have influenced fashions, like the Kashmiri shawl in courtly France; interiors, such as upholstery in chintz, originally *kalamkari* from Masulipatnam; trading patterns across the old Silk Route from China to the Middle East; and politics, with Mahatma Gandhi encouraging hand-spun, handwoven fabric, *khadi*, as a symbol of India's fight for freedom from colonialism and towards self-reliance.

There are statistics that show that the number of handloom weavers in India has drastically reduced and that the younger generation does not want to practise the craft carried on by their families for generations. Challenges are also faced from the power loom and mechanized sector. Western fashion has lately influenced Indian women in urbanized areas away from wearing traditional textiles, and many have changed their lifestyles and home décor from traditional Indian settings to more cosmopolitan, universal ones. While changes are bound to occur over decades in the natural processes of the evolution of society and technology, there are many positive movements too, such as a return to a contemporary form of Indian-ness and experiments and explorations with the very nature and techniques used in making hand-worked textiles. Today, there is a growing realization that they offer an Indian style of uniqueness that can merge beautifully with cosmopolitan décor, just as Indian fabrics being highlighted in the Indian fashion industry brought noticeable attention to them as exclusive and unique, especially embroideries, handloom weaving and block printing.

As an independent India grows away from the yoke and influences of colonialism, there is a growing realization that the craft

PREVIOUS PAGES
A detail of the Ras-Rang tapestry for "Suhana," which demonstrates multiple craft techniques.
Image credit: Spider Design

RIGHT
This piece is an original creation of the well-known Tree of Life motif for a special project linking crafts and calligraphy. The design is executed through a combination of art and phrases in the Telugu script, demonstrating the potential of *kalamkari* textile art.
Image credit: Dastkari Haat Samiti

practitioners of India are very much alive and well, and their vast repository of skills offers immense possibilities for architects and interior designers to tap—through collaborations and a merging of contemporary ideas with old craft techniques.

Indian brocades and carpets have been known for generations, but new innovations are happening almost every day. Young textile designers and dye experts from rural areas have not only collaborated to revive dying skills but have also created new techniques and textures with a variety of metallic yarn and fresh colour palettes. Colours from various natural ingredients alter with each region. The world is slowly waking up to the possibilities of bespoke colours being created for limited editions of fabrics for those who appreciate that elements such as water, sun and air interact on natural dyes differently. They are learning to see beauty in non-standardized results and energy-reducing processes. Container-loads of thousands of metres of the same fabric are no longer in demand, when a limited edition of something custom-made works better for appreciative clients.

Individual projects involve intimate collaborations, combining the creativity and unbound vision of professional architects and interior designers with the creators of handmade fabrics. The reverse is equally true.

Craftspeople have innate skills and know their techniques intricately. When these skills are stirred up by designers, their imagination flowers with a new freedom. Similarly, craft techniques understood by the modern professional enable new possibilities for adaptation and applications.

The use of Indian handcrafted textiles in both heritage and contemporary interiors has always lent a special edge to the work, something that is not easily available in other countries. Each body of work becomes an exclusive, un-replicable expression, a new creation in that moment of common understanding, and a fusion of new ideas and old techniques. While the West has well-preserved heritage properties that show not only their own craft but also those appropriated from Asian countries, especially India, it is India that stands alone in offering excellent handcrafted textiles in the present day. The existence of indomitable weavers who never gave up their skills is a treasure waiting to be explored to its fullest.

Inspirations for the use of Indian textiles in interiors come from a number of Asian and Middle Eastern origins, such as decorative temporary tents, which recall the Persian and desert styles of yore. The *kanaat* (a tented enclosure), erected for weddings or religious festivals, calls for elaborate embellishments motivated purely out of devotion for the occasion. The display of imaginative flair and talent offers new ideas to urban designers ordinarily used to less tactile structures. A young woman has demonstrated her skills at converting handwoven pieces of *gamchha*, the all-purpose towel for the working class, incidentally woven by women, to show how a majestic celebratory tent in appliqué can adorn entire walls and ceilings. A more sophisticated rendering of a residential tent in a hotel resort shows the talents of block printers of Rajasthan.

A little-known "wonder weave" emerges from a few looms under the expertise of master weavers in Varanasi, where peacocks abound. The shed feathers are collected, carefully

Jamdani weaving in Bengal is a shadow play between muslin fabric and a double weft patterning. Jamdani is often created for saris or fine curtains. Image credit: Dastkari Haat Samiti

The Samode Palace in Rajasthan has extensions providing tented accommodation to guests in which the entire interior is enriched with decorative textiles. Image credit: Pradeep Sachdeva Design Associates

separated strand by strand and spun into yarn that shimmers, just as the feathers do when displayed by a peacock. The yarn is woven on the weavers' ancient handlooms into upholstery cloth and sold at high prices to wealthy sheikhs in the Middle East. This is obviously produced in limited quantities to ensure the safety of the royal birds. The very same weaver has created an entirely new technique to replicate a magical-looking butterfly as a motif for an order of cushion covers from a Spanish client. Similarly, women *kantha* weavers of Bengal have been inspired by an Italian interior designer to create finely embroidered yardage and bedcovers in contemporary designs, quite different from the figures and flowers employed in the traditional quilts the women embroidered for their own use.

Mountain and desert pastoralists and farming communities in remote areas of India are today using local fibres to create textiles that offer comfort, for usage as upholstery and floor coverings, offering new textures and materials such as camel hair, hemp and jute. All these are highly sustainable, rapidly renewable fibres that not only offer new alternatives to interior designers but also provide livelihoods to thousands. Natural fibres are strong and versatile and have been developed for commercial use in interiors by textile engineers and researchers in the past 20 years.

A fascinating exercise has been taking place in the tiny hill state of Meghalaya, in north-east India. The ramie plant, *Boehmeria nivea*, used by locals to make fishing nets and eaten as a cooked vegetable, was developed by the state in collaboration with French textile technologists not only into fashion fabrics but also into upholstery coverings. Its fibres are stronger than cotton, linen and wool, and are moisture-absorbent, mildew-resistant and resist fading in strong sunlight.

Jute is another wonder grass that morphs from simple burlap to textured, organic-looking coverings, ranging from carpets and rugs, upholstery and curtains, and accessories such as cushion covers. Since jute is cultivated in vast quantities in India, it can be applied in many creative ways, such as using jute strings to create hanging lamps or seating, when combined with bamboo or wood. Its natural shades range from light creamy browns to pale coffee. Current trends towards a more minimalistic, organic interior do not feel welcoming towards the more vibrant traditional hues of Indian handlooms, but this is where these textured grasses come into play and offer a new variety of subtle, unobtrusive hues. Jute fabric can also be dyed in natural dyes to give a gentle, antique effect. The large range of vibrant *durrie*s woven in Mirzapur, Navalgund,

This elegantly upholstered chair has been created out of a wonder grass called ramie, which can be converted into fabric for use in interiors or for high fashion. Such new textile engineering points to a more sustainable ecology for interiors.
Image credit: Jaya Jaitly

Telangana and Bengal have enabled low-cost and simple but aesthetically decorated homes to enjoy floor coverings that enrich the room and are easy to maintain. Handloom weavers have become good designers, innovators and skilled imitators of Persian *kilim*s. They weave classic film posters and calligraphy designs onto carpets. They are now venturing into furniture production by creating poufs and ottoman covers woven in the *durrie* technique. Since technology has enabled the softening of what is essentially a coarse fabric used for sacks, the use of jute in design has seen a flowering of inspired applications.

Tourism is expanding exponentially under new concepts such as responsible tourism and sustainable tourism. These have given opportunities for local interior designers to highlight crafts and textiles from their own regions. Incorporating them into the décor of local resorts, boutique hotels, refurbished heritage properties, tourism centres and state guesthouses helps to display their roots and local talents as well as provide livelihoods for rural craftspeople. The Khyber Himalayan Resort and Spa in the snowy heights of Gulmarg, in Kashmir, displays every kind of crewel embroidery in its décor throughout the establishment. Many north-eastern states of India, with their many kinds of weaves created on home-based looms by women, are also new attractions for tourists. Many have realized that to attract tourists looking for a real difference, it is local handcrafted work that lends uniqueness and character to their establishments.

Finally, one must bow to historic architecture that has influenced textile designs, as in Chanderi, Madhya Pradesh, where the lattice work on old buildings has inspired contemporary public benches and fabric woven by local weavers. A study of old carved statues and multiple facets in ancient forests and palaces, and even traditional community structures in bamboo, can serve as new sources of inspiration for architects and interior designers in future bodies of work. Whether inspirations are old or new, it is the unique and exclusive skills of the crafted textile sector that offer it freely. •

Textiles

Kalamkari is a traditional technique of hand-painting fabric using organic dyes, practised in India mainly in the southern Indian states of Andhra Pradesh and Telangana, with the town of Srikalahasti being a major hub. Dyes are used in a runny consistency to paint lyrical forms on fabric. Popular themes include narratives from mythological epics as well as motifs drawn from nature.

Inspiration: The client operates a flagship airport store showcasing traditional art and craft products from southern India. Hence, the use of *kalamkari* for a textile canopy created an artistic synergy with the language of the store. The canopy was created using 49 panels, each of 2m x 1m dimension. Inspired by local flora and fauna, the pieces use earthy natural dyes. Further, the cascading panels feature extensive, intricate artwork, and create impactful perspectives.

Sustainability: The materials are handwoven fabrics of cotton and silk, and dyes derived from natural ingredients that are free of chemicals. By showcasing the craft and the communities involved, in the middle of a bustling airport, such design interventions help create sustainable livelihoods. ■

Material: Fabric, organic dyes
Technique: *Kalamkari* painting
Craftsperson(s): Traditional artists from the *kalamkari*-based NGO Dwarka, Bengaluru.
Source Region: Andhra Pradesh, India
Studio: Siddhartha Das Studio

Textiles

Furnishing, being an important segment of interiors, aims to impart a unique identity to the space. These curtain designs were developed in detail to fit the technical requirements of machine embroidery craft in different stages. Further, selecting thread colours and appropriate stitches (*taanka*s) also played a vital role in getting the desired look and texture. These embroidered fabrics were curated to complement the embroidery work. They were pre-cut and made ready with manual markings to pass through the machines accurately. After all these rigorous processes, the final embroidered fabrics were stitched by tailors to cast curtains and installed at the site with carefully taken measurements.

Inspiration: Gujarat is an exceptional place for the embroidery craft. Following the core theme of the residence, inspired by artist S.H. Raza's work and patterns, curtain designs are embellished by using the traditional embroidery craft. Raza's *bindu*, lines and triangles are beautifully bedecked and composed on fabrics by colourful threads of machine embroidery, hand embroidery and *khatli* work of Surat. The beautiful craft of embroidery is full of expressions and has had a great impact on human lifestyle since ages. The colourful threads, interesting stitches, *taanka*s, with beautiful weaves of fabrics, create magic.

Sustainability: Many people in Gujarat, in urban as well as rural areas, still depend on their age-old embroidery heritage. This idea of textile customization for the interiors can surely open up doors of opportunity and employment for embroidery craftsmen. The artisans involved in this project were all local craftsmen and skilful Gujarati women who have kept alive this thread craft as a part of their tradition. Surat, being the textile hub of Gujarat and a source of machine embroidery, has many experienced artisans, making it easy to source both material and talent locally. ■

Material: Textiles
Technique: Embroidery and *khatli* work
Craftsperson(s): Gulambhai Jariwala/Royal Embroidery, Ehsanali Shaikh (*khatli* work)
Source Region: Gujarat, India
Studio: Filigree Fabriculture, Surat

Textiles

The traditional craft of appliqué has been employed in creating light fixtures and lamps for this office space, in the conference room on the ground floor and in the offices on the fourth floor, at times becoming abstractions of the various animals that were said to be aboard Noah's Ark, at others bearing a resemblance to the sails on a boat. Apart from this, an installation designed and executed by the artist Mrugen Rathod, called "Avataran," also using appliqué, depicts the course of the Vishwamitri River as it runs through Vadodara, speaking to ideas of urbanity and development.

Inspiration: In a formal space that integrates within it various ideas and forms of art—both modern and traditional—this material and its usage adds softness to the interiors, juxtaposing against wood, metal and other heavy materials used to create spaces within the office. It provides a sense of opposite ideas coming together, not contradicting one another, and creating a sense of balance. In a seemingly disconnected

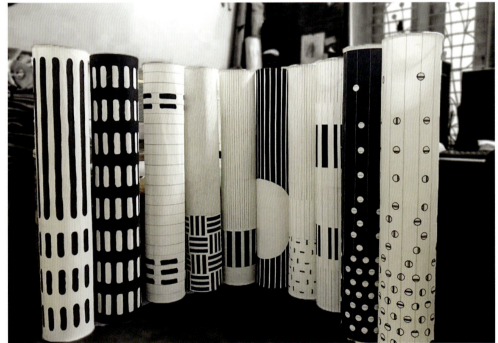

space, this element provides a sense of fluidity and continuity.

Sustainability: The conversation has been geared towards sustainability of a craft, and the exploration of alternate avenues for its expression in today's times. In doing so, the space has expanded not only the purpose and ability of the craft but also the very meaning of the word "sustainability." ■

Material: Textiles
Technique: Appliqué
Craftsperson(s): Mrugen Rathod (artist), Mehr Seth, Rajesh Sharma (appliqué)
Source Region: N.A.
Studio: M/s. Prabhakar B. Bhagwat

Textiles

This design solution used silk as the base fabric, upon which batik processes were done to bring out a floral theme for furnishing elements in the design, in keeping with the teachings of the Mother of Auroville. The fabric used was Bangalore silk and the artisans were from central India. Detailed graphics were created and then worked on by hand to capture all details. Embroidery and other embellishments were used to enhance the designs before installation.

Inspiration: The clients were followers of Sri Aurobindo and the Mother and hence the design was conceived to connect with their beliefs. The Significance of Flowers, a teaching by the Mother, was chosen as the theme and batik was chosen as the medium of expression. Batik allowed for the floral theme to achieve full expression through vibrant colours and fluidity of lines.

Sustainability: Batik is a very eco-friendly medium for art. In most cases, natural dyes are used. There is almost no environmental damage done in the process. Materials used in this are also easily accessible and cause no health issues to the artisans. ■

Material: Silk
Technique: Batik
Craftsperson(s): Jaba Champaneria
Source Region: Central India
Studio: OBL/QUE | ESSTEAM | Urban Initiatives

Textiles • 137

Textiles

Taking inspiration from the native flora and fauna of the place, special woodcutting blocks were made by printmaker Dhvani Behl, borrowing from Japanese woodblock printmaking. Thereafter, in homage to regional influences, large, woodcut themes of neem and babul trees were hand-printed on pre-stitched fabric to create tented design solutions.

Inspiration: The area is full of captivating flora and fauna, and even serves as a popular bird-watching site. Taking inspiration from this, nature themes were chosen for the design in soft, organic fabrics. As a result, woodblock printing was employed innovatively to create a vibrant canvas celebrating the biodiversity of plant and animal species that surround the property. This method of bringing nature into the interiors manifests as an extension of the animal sightings observed in the environs.

Sustainability: Exploring the scalability of the age-old craft tradition of woodcutting in a contemporary mould was an attempt to celebrate its impact and sustain its relevance in novel ways. The applied crafts were also taught to a few locals, in order to work with them on capacity building and skill development. ■

Material: Fabric, wood
Technique: Woodcuts on fabric
Craftsperson(s): Dhvani Behl (Flora for Fauna)
Source Region: Rajasthan and Uttar Pradesh, India
Studio: Studio Lotus

Textiles

The Japanese techniques of paper folding (origami) and paper cutting (*kirigami*) transfer very well to parchment leather (goatskin leather). These techniques are fused with Indian pictographic representation techniques, sub-divided onto the folded surfaces, as well as traditional punching techniques, creating sparkles of light. Parchment leather has a stunning opalescent glow when light passes through the material. Reclaimed leather is stretched and sun-dried, before being cleaned and burnished by artisans and leather workers. Then, the leather is scored, folded and punched to mould the desired forms to create sparkles of light.

Inspiration: The traditional craft of shadow puppetry in Andhra Pradesh, also called *tholu bommalata*, plays with the idea of light and shadow in a two-dimensional medium. The Japanese paper arts of origami and *kirigami* also play with light and shadow in three dimensions. Fusing these two together allows us to merge these two cultures together into a new, universal language of facets, colour and light—all inspired by the forms and geometry of nature.

Sustainability: Animal husbandry is widely practised all over India, making goatskin leather easy to procure, as small-scale husbandry uses all parts of the animal while respecting the environment. Moreover, this is not done at an industrial scale; it is done in small clusters of goat herders in harmony with grazing lands of a village or community. Not only is the reclaimed leather sustainably sourced from such local clusters, but it is also a very durable material if given a little regular care. ■

Material: Parchment leather/goatskin leather, knitted wool
Technique: *Tholu bommalata* (India), origami and *kirigami* (Japan)
Craftsperson(s): Neha Bhardwaj (knitting)
Source Region: Andhra Pradesh, India
Studio: Oritecture/Ankon Mitra

Textiles

Indian crafts, especially textile crafts, tend to have a strong regional flavour. For this project, it was desired to project an identity of integrated "Indian-ness," which is why we decided to combine several different styles of textile work from across the country. Embroidery from Kashmir, *kantha* work, patchwork, hand appliqué, screen printing and machine-guided appliqué were all used by craftspersons from Rajasthan, Bihar, Gujarat and Delhi to create a niche expression to tell the story of India in a subtle way. Although each element retains a strong distinctive identity, they were brought together to create a compelling and beautiful narrative element within the spatial aesthetic.

Inspiration: Given the large variety in textile crafts across India, it seemed like the perfect choice to create a storytelling narrative of Indian-ness. It not only allowed various crafts to tell a story but also brought various craftspersons across the country together to create a cohesive design using their own shared but different design vocabulary.

Sustainability: The fabrics used are available across the country and hence can be sourced locally for all such projects. Moreover, these materials are naturally sustainable with azo-free dyeing techniques. Being textiles-based, these designs can be easily maintained and upcycled or reused in time. ■

Material: Silk, satin
Technique: Embroidery, patchwork, *kantha*, appliqué, screen printing
Craftsperson(s): GVCS, Barmer and Abhudaya, New Delhi
Source Region: All over India
Studio: Spider Design

Textiles

Traditionally painted Mata ni Pachhedi images were graphically composed and digitally printed on yardage to provide embellishment to the banquet hall and other prominent areas. Similarly, contemporized images were used to create digitally printed wallpaper for the kids' area.

Inspiration: The theme of nature and goddess worship that permeates the ethos of Mata ni Pachhedi art was appealing. The new setting gave the craft a different context and enabled its application and use in a modern setting, while still retaining its traditional essence.

Sustainability: There is a strong element of social sustainability as this project enabled this dying art to be used and applied in a new setting. ■

Material: Fabric, paper
Technique: Mata ni Pachhedi painting
Source Region: Gujarat, India
Studio: House of MG

Textiles

The client, Shriji Arvindsinghji Mewar of the H.R.H. Group of Hotels, wanted to expand and upgrade an existing hotel into a larger resort. Primary construction was of local stone while bricks were occasionally used in the masonry in partition walls. However, the inner linings of the stone walls were in brick to facilitate electrical and plumbing works. Large spans were roofed with stone patties resting on mild steel girders on the lower flanges. Long and wide *jharokha*s were required to accommodate extra sleeping areas, hence projected by more than three-and-a-half feet using large stone brackets and mild steel sections. The verandah was designed to be an extension of the guest room as a logical response to the character and ambience of the site. All the furniture and soft furnishings were designed around the local foliage and wildlife. Curtains, bed linen and cushion covers were screen-printed on cotton and satin, and the woollen runners were handwoven with tiger-stripe patterns and paw prints in the wildlife-themed rooms. Craftsmen who had built the earlier structure were recalled from their villages to execute the project.

Inspiration: The basis for the architectural language of this project was the local typology of construction in local stone, with *jharokha*s and thatched roofs, and building as per the contours of the land to minimize cutting of rocks.

Sustainability: Use of local materials and craftsmen proved to be economical and convenient, especially in an isolated spot like Kumbhalgarh. It also succeeded in giving the project a rare quality of timelessness. ■

Material: Stone, brick, steel
Technique: Stone masonry, screen printing
Source Region: Rajasthan, India
Studio: Abhikram Architects

Textiles • 145

SURFACE DECORATION

Changing the Writing on the Wall

SURFACE DECORATION

Changing the Writing on the Wall

• Mitchell Abdul Karim Crites

It was around 1988 when Jangarh Singh Shyam, the legendary Pardhan Gond artist, came to our house in Delhi to show his latest work. He pulled out of his handmade *khadi*-lined folder wonderful black-and-white drawings and colourful paintings of trees, creatures and gods, goddesses and demons, all deeply rooted in his tribal traditions. They were profoundly original and pulsating with life and energy but they were all quite small. I rarely intervened in Jangarh's work, but this time I thought I might hazard a suggestion.

I told him in America we have a concept in art that we call "wall power." He was intrigued and asked what it meant. I said that some artists, not all, can paint BIG! He then wanted to know if I thought he had wall power. I said I was sure he could conceptualize and paint on a grand scale and that I had already bought large sheets of paper and rolls of canvas for him to take back to his home in Bhopal to practise on. Two months later, he returned and shyly unveiled his latest works of art. In an instant, soaring trees-of-life, commanding deities and majestic antlered deer transformed our drawing room into a mysterious world that summoned up the very roots of Indian civilization. And, just a year later, Jangarh was invited to paint a massive mural at the epic "Magicians of the Earth" show at the Centre Pompidou, in Paris, proclaiming to the world that a major talent had indeed emerged.

In the more than three decades that have passed since that conversation with Jangarh, I have worked and collaborated with many other indigenous artists, as well as those trained in various classical traditions, and have come to realize that traditional Indian artists and artisans possess a remarkable ability to augment the scale of their artistic vision, enabling them to cover large surfaces with often spectacular results. For many years, I've wondered how they can do this and with such inner cultural confidence. Often untutored, untrained and with no strong visual tradition, the artists seem to draw from an inherent interior reservoir of memory and imagination, which motivates and inspires them—a kind of "Design DNA."

They also observe, from childhood, members of the family painting elaborate decorative motifs on the mud floors and walls of their village homes during rituals and festivals or just for the sheer joy of decoration. And, whether they lived on the plains or in the forest, when they stepped outside their homes, the vista stretched far beyond the village, uninterrupted, into the distant horizon. India has also been for millennia a place where grand and monumental architecture has been part of the landscape. During pilgrimages and travels, artists and their families would visit and draw inspiration from magnificent temples, palaces, forts, tombs and majestic ruins decorated with a wealth of geometric and floral patterns, creatures, birds and a pantheon of tribal and classical deities. In the same way that the *dastangoi* storytellers can weave with words the epic stories of the past, so can these traditional artists create on a similar grand scale and on any surface they are asked to work on.

The extraordinarily rich Pardhan Gond tradition of painting is, of course, but one of the folk, tribal and traditional art forms that lend themselves to "wall power with soul." Important and ground-breaking creations are also being produced by the Warli artists of Maharashtra, the Pithora painters of central and western India, as well as the powerful graphic designs emerging from the Mithila and Hazaribagh

PREVIOUS PAGES
A traditional painter works on a large painting in the Warli style, showing influences from Pithora painting.
Image credit: Mapin

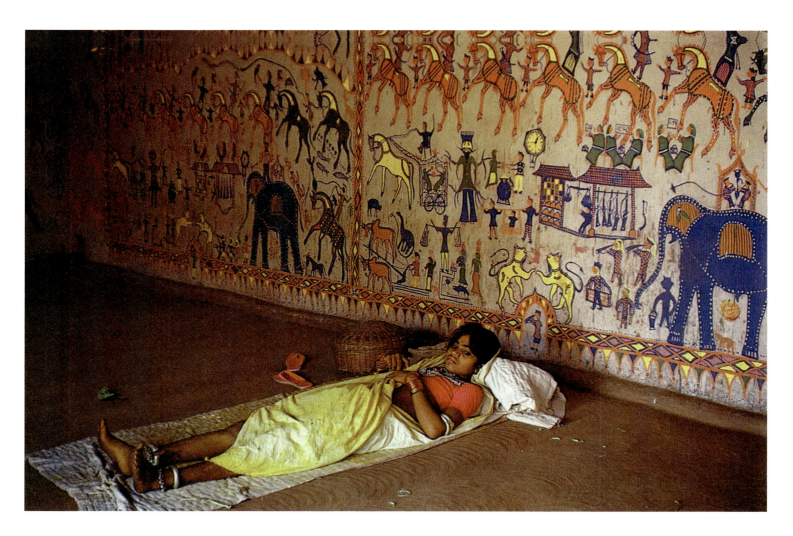

This photograph shows a traditional Pithora wall mural, depicting the wedding procession of the local deity Pithora, on his way to marry Pithori. Ritual paintings such as these are believed to offer protection to the inhabitants of the dwelling.
Image credit: Mapin

traditions of Bihar and Jharkhand, as each artist finds their own original voice.

In this short essay, I will focus on four very different projects, which will demonstrate the degree of wall power that these remarkable traditional artists possess. They include a state legislature, a mosque, a private mansion and a restored 18th-century water palace. Two are in India and two abroad, in order to demonstrate that projects around the world have begun to recognize the power of Indian traditional design, art and craftsmanship.

Vidhan Bhavan, Bhopal

Vidhan Bhavan, a grand and ambitious complex to house the state legislative assembly of Madhya Pradesh, perched atop the Arera Hill in Bhopal, was designed by one of India's greatest architects, Charles Correa, and completed in 1993. In a visionary step, the government commissioned Jangarh Singh Shyam to decorate the walls of one of the interior courtyards. By this time, Jangarh was recognized as one of the finest and most creative indigenous artists in the country as well as abroad. I can still see him lying on his back on tall and rickety bamboo scaffolding, reminiscent of Michelangelo painting the Sistine Chapel. Slowly, Gond gods and leaping tigers majestically filled the space. It was a true expression of wall power, suffused with feeling and primordial energy that had for so long lain latent within him, waiting for a space big enough to showcase his protean creativity.

Two of the leading scholars on Jangarh Singh Shyam have recorded their thoughts on the power, scale and originality of these extraordinary wall murals.

Surface Decoration • 149

Dr Aurogeeta Das: "Jangarh's murals at the Vidhan Bhavan match the grandeur of Correa's architecture with, for example, his paintings of a ferocious tiger and an awe-inspiring Gond deity, while the detailed pattern in his conception—especially in the flora and fauna depicted—simultaneously provides an effective foil to the monumental expanse of Correa's walls."

From *The Enchanted Forest: Paintings and Drawings from the Crites Collection*

Dr Jyotindra Jain: "According to Jangarh, the vast and alluring painterly space of the murals not only anticipated and determined the large scale of the images but also seduced him to add new ones, such as the colossal airplane, the gigantic tiger and the majestic bird about to take flight."

From *Jangarh Singh Shyam: The Conjuror's Archive*

Wall paintings by Jangarh Singh Shyam, Vidhan Bhavan, Bhopal. © Charles Correa Archives, Mumbai

I remember when the project was finished, Jangarh came to Delhi and told me how proud he was of the work he had done at the Vidhan Bhavan and that they had paid him seven lakhs. I remember thinking it should have been much more but it established once and for all his reputation as a leading contemporary artist with "wall power and soul," who had far transcended his folk and tribal roots, and the spectacular murals inspired a whole new generation of Pardhan Gond artists to broaden their own creative vision.

Grand Mansion of Shri Lakshmi Mittal, London

Two grand mansions built in 1847 in Italianate palazzo style had stood empty for a number of years on one of the most prestigious tree-lined avenues in central London until a visionary Iranian art collector and businessman, David Khalili, saw the opportunity of a lifetime. He purchased 18–19 Kensington Palace Gardens in the early nineties and immediately broke down the walls that had always separated them, turning them into one of the grandest houses in the city.

Khalili, a connoisseur of Mughal art and architecture, had long admired the classical styles of decoration, which had ornamented the Taj Mahal and other great Mughal buildings of the 16th and 17th centuries. I remember him saying at the beginning of the project, "We want to plug into the amazing historic and cultural legacy of the Taj Mahal and use the greatest artisans working today, especially those who can trace their ancestry back to this legendary building. The scale will be epic, grand and monumental but I'm sure that they can rise to the occasion." And they did. More than 400 master artists, ornamentalists, stone carvers and inlay artisans were brought together to conceptualize and create this amazing project from 1996 to 1999. At the time, the refurbishment was believed to have been second in scale only to the restoration of Windsor Castle following the 1992 fire.

The spectacular underground swimming pool was inlaid like a Persian carpet, with precious stone and coloured marble, and shaded by white marble *jaali*s carved with the same geometry as the Taj Mahal. The master bathroom suites were embellished with sliced amethyst and mother-of-pearl in cascades of wisteria and red agate roses. Twelve white marble panels titled "The Seasons" graced the walls of the Orangerie, each panel measuring four metres in height and inlaid with precious stone, depicting flowering trees filled with nesting birds, which were in bloom in London during the different months of the year. They were conceived and painted by the master watercolour artist Michael Giles, and then reinterpreted for classical inlay by S. G. Ranjan in Delhi, one of the finest ornamentalists working today, so that the delicate detail of each petal and branch could be precisely expressed in precious stone by master inlay artisans. It was a wonderful fusion of East and West, which has always inspired so much of Mughal art and architecture.

In 2004, 18-19 Kensington Palace Gardens was purchased by the steel magnate Shri Lakshmi Mittal for the highest price ever paid for a private home at that time. Clearly, the legend of the Taj Mahal and the skill of Indian master artisans had attracted him. Such projects are important because they give work to so many skilled artisans, while keeping the art and craft traditions alive and, at the same time, challenging the artists and artisans to push their creative boundaries as far as they can possibly go.

Federal Territory Mosque, Kuala Lumpur

The design and decoration of contemporary mosques have, over the last 50 years, been a catalyst for bringing together artists, artisans and calligraphers from around the world who share design ideas and traditional techniques of craftsmanship. Among the grandest and most beautiful is the Federal Territory Mosque of Kuala Lumpur, perched dramatically on a hill in one of the suburbs of the capital, and completed in the year 2000. More than 350 stone carvers and inlay artisans from India were commissioned to create the powerful calligraphy and ornamentation for the *qibla* prayer wall and the imposing entrance gateway.

One of the biggest challenges facing designers in any project is where should they draw their inspiration from. The government officials said they preferred a floral theme, as opposed to strict geometry, which was agreeable to me since Malaysia is a land of flowers—found in abundance in both urban manicured gardens and the thick and lush vegetation of the jungle. I remember asking which flowers they preferred and they said roses, gladioli and carnations, none of which is indigenous to Malaysia. We then gently suggested to the Prime Minister that perhaps we could explore the local flowering plants and trees of Malaysia, which could be stylized and drawn in a traditional Islamic style suitable for carving and inlay.

The powers that be agreed with the proposal, and S. G. Ranjan, who had already worked on the Mittal Mansion in London, created stylized drawings of the flowers so that they could be carved and inlaid with precious stone into white marble. The majestic interior prayer wall measures 28 metres in height and is inlaid with more than half a million individual pieces of cut precious stone. We also created beautiful gardens surrounding the mosque and planted the same flowering plants and trees so visitors and the faithful who came to pray could see indigenous Malaysian flowers in both art and nature.

Jal Mahal, Jaipur

For the last hundred years, the image of the early 18th-century Jal Mahal, floating in the Man Sagar Lake on the road leading from the Pink City of Jaipur to the legendary palace fortress of Amber, remained poignantly grand but profoundly in need of restoration. The lake had nearly dried up and the elegant pavilions were crumbling. Through the enlightened patronage of local jeweller, philanthropist and lover of art Shri Navratan Kothari, the Jal Mahal was slowly and painstakingly brought back to life.

Lippan kaam, or relief work, using a mixture of mud and dung embellished with mirrors and glass, is a technique of decoration seen commonly in western India.
Image credit: Mapin

Jaipur is truly a city of artists, and many of its great masters can trace their ancestry back to the legendary kingdoms of Central Asia and the Mughal capitals of Delhi, Agra and Fatehpur Sikri. Each *mohalla* of the city is inhabited by artisans practising and selling their individual wares. While exploring the back lanes of the Pink City, I discovered more than 150 flourishing art and craft traditions, including kite making, metalworking, stone carving, mirror-work, musical instruments and even an old *haveli* where leopards, lions and tigers were trained for the entertainment of the Jaipur royal family.

The Jal Mahal Project, begun in 2007, brought together several hundred of these master artists and artisans to work on the restoration of the main building and the surrounding lake and shore land. The pavilions were restored and repainted and in the uppermost courtyard, the Chameli Bagh, a magnificent water garden, the finest built in northern India for the last 150 years, was constructed using the skills of master stone carvers, specialists in water technology and traditional gardeners. The aquatic ecosystem of the lake came back to life, and local and migratory birds returned.

The interior walls of the winding corridors were painted by local artists, who were delighted to find grand spaces where they could once again practise their art. Gilded floral decoration, painted peacocks and banana plants now grace these walls.

The ability of the artists and artisans to cover large surfaces with originality and vitality was extraordinary. And why not? They had been exposed their entire lives to the grand decoration of Amber Fort and the Jaipur City Palace. Scale did not intimidate them, and the magnificent luxury for which Jaipur has always been known has once again been displayed on the walls of the Jal Mahal.

> To restore a building is not to preserve or rebuild it. It is to reinstate it in a condition of completeness which could never have existed at any given time.
> —Violette Leduc

In conclusion, I would like to stress we all need to recognize that tribal, folk, traditional and classical artists and artisans, from one end of India to the other, possess an extraordinary talent, which allows them not only to work on a large scale, but also with an endless variety of materials and techniques. They have no need to slavishly copy but are capable of independent and highly original creativity. To put it simply, they have "wall power with soul."

If all of us just added in our projects even 10 or 15 per cent of work done by these gifted masters, these endangered and precious traditions could be revived and passed on to the next generation and, in the process, the lives of each artist and artisan and their families would be significantly improved in multiple ways. All they need is work. •

Surface Decoration

While this art form has been seen independently creating narratives pertaining to the community from which it has originated, in the context of the office space, the Gond wall art creates a modern interpretation and narrates the story of Noah's Ark. It works in conjunction with the various other art forms such as appliqué, woodwork, metalwork and concrete that make up the space. The medium and scale in which the art form has been expressed distinguishes it from conventional manners and processes of use. While many Gond artists today have stopped using traditional stone or vegetable dye colour and often use paints as available in shops, the technique itself is endemic to this art form.

Inspiration: Traditionally, Gond artists use lines and motifs in order to convey a sense of movement within still images, narrating stories of their surroundings, their communities and circumstances. In this office space, three adjoining walls have become a visual representation of the story of Noah's Ark—a grey background with silver art work at the fore. The motifs of this artform seemed best suited to convey this story, which is further enhanced by being written in the Devanagari script. Since the art is spread over three walls, it is simultaneously open to interpretation and then becomes absolute, depending on where one approaches the story from.

Sustainability: The project examines another contiguous idea of sustainability, one that incorporates the ideas of these art forms into everyday spaces, giving them an alternative sense of purpose—bringing together ideas of functionality and usability. It creates new opportunities for tribal artists, in this case the Gond artists, to express their work in contemporary settings where it is not facile decoration but integral to the narrative of the space. ■

Material: Paints
Technique: Gond wall art
Craftsperson(s): Kaushal Prasad Tekam
Source Region: Madhya Pradesh, India
Studio: M/s. Prabhakar B. Bhagwat

Surface Decoration

Surface Decoration

The Gonds are a community in central India, with their own vibrant style of painting. In the Gond belief system, their art, with its depiction of natural elements, is a sacred reflection of the close relationship between people and nature. For this reason, traditional Gond painting often features trees, animals and birds, reflecting the rich biodiversity of the central Indian jungles. The artwork is typically executed with natural pigments, charcoal, leaves and soil, among other materials.

Inspiration: Since the Gonds believe that viewing a beautiful image begets good luck, they often decorate their houses with traditional paintings. Taking this idea into a contemporary home, especially one filled with abundant natural light and verdant greenery, the idea of Gond painting seemed like a superior alternative to wallpaper or other methods of wall paint. A few rough sketches were done on paper to finalize the concept, after which the wall was painted with acrylic colours by Gond artists from Madhya Pradesh. Black-and-white elements were finished first, followed by details in colour.

Sustainability: The simplicity of the mural complements the simplicity of the craft itself, which only needs a few colours and brushes to execute. No maintenance is required, other than washing once in a while with mild soap, which can keep the walls clean without harming the artwork. ■

Material: Acrylic paint on wall surface
Technique: Gond painting
Craftsperson(s): Dilip Shyam
Source Region: Madhya Pradesh, India
Studio: Pankaj Vaid Architects

Surface Decoration

Surface Decoration

The scenography of the Jal Mahal in Jaipur was intended to evoke the courtly arts of 18th-century Rajasthan. Miniature painting, being an important art form, was chosen for the decoration of this space. Flowers found at various historic monuments in Jaipur were hand-drawn by the designer and executed on the walls by traditional artisans. During the day, sunlight filters in through the large arched openings, making the gold-coloured creepers and vibrant flowers glow like jewels.

Inspiration: The Jal Mahal celebrates the courtly arts of 18th-century Rajasthan. Jaipur is an important centre of miniature painting, with many artists who continue this legacy of painting. Hence, this traditional art form was chosen to evoke the bygone era of courtly Rajasthan and to pay homage to the local artistic and architectural legacy of Jaipur.

Sustainability: The pigments themselves are non-invasive. Moreover, they can be sanded away or whitewashed with no damage to the original structure or on surrounding ecological landscape. It also showcases the skills of the traditional artists, thus helping to create sustainable livelihoods. ■

Material: Natural pigments
Technique: Traditional miniature painting
Source Region: Rajasthan, India
Studio: Siddhartha Das Studio with Mitchell Crites and Deependra Singh (conceptualization and coordination of painting masters)

Surface Decoration • 159

Surface Decoration

The vibrant art of Rajasthani miniature painting was incorporated in the design to preserve the authenticity and richness of the traditional Rajasthani *haveli*s and palaces. Skilled local artists were chosen for this project. They made preliminary sketches on paper and then converted them into stencils in order to transfer the design onto the wall surfaces. The paint used was a mixture of stone pigments and acrylic colours, in order to give a long-lasting finish. In certain sections, gold and silver foil were also used to add a regal touch to the ambience.

Inspiration: The inspiration for this design comes from the Mewar school of miniature painting, characterized by vivid colours and emotional appeal. The wall paintings add an essence of royal aesthetics but also permit the artisans to unfold a narrative and tell stories with every brushstroke.

Sustainability: The ingenuity of mixing stone pigments with acrylic paint not only provides a greener and safer option for large-scale wall paintings but also requires minimal maintenance and lasts a long time. ∎

Material: Natural pigments
Technique: Rajasthani miniature painting
Craftsperson(s): Zenul Khan
Source Region: Rajasthan, India
Studio: Chirag Shah and Associates

Surface Decoration • 161

Surface Decoration

This Madhubani painting adorns a 35-feet lift shaft in a home. A mundane lift shaft was converted into a central element of the courtyard, connecting three storeys, by painting it in the traditional motifs of Madhubani painting. This was done by Team Rogan as a free-hand drawing in sections by climbing into the lift car and over the scaffolding.

Inspiration: The vision of converting a mundane lift shaft into a piece of art called for an intervention that camouflaged the exposed mechanisms with applied artwork. The client was an admirer of nature and nature drawings and hence organic forms, such as the "Tree of Life" motif, were chosen. The curvilinear art of Madhubani was a perfect fit, given the various blooming flowers and chirping birds that were planned. Thus, inspirations from the past and present came together to create a stunning home décor element.

Sustainability: The paints used in this project were water-soluble acrylics, which are non-toxic and resistant to wear and tear, as opposed to high-end paints, which have harsh chemicals and require regular upkeep. Also, by keeping the artistic skills of craftspersons alive, the project provided social and artistic sustainability. ■

Material: Water-soluble acrylic paints
Technique: Madhubani wall painting
Source Region: Bihar, India
Studio: Aangan Architects, with Team Rogan

Surface Decoration • 163

Surface Decoration

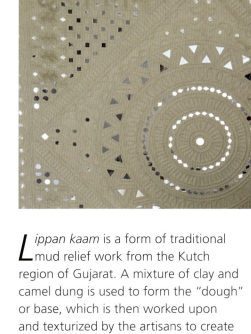

Lippan kaam is a form of traditional mud relief work from the Kutch region of Gujarat. A mixture of clay and camel dung is used to form the "dough" or base, which is then worked upon and texturized by the artisans to create designs. Following this, small pieces of mirrored glass, called *aabhla*, are affixed to the design in intricate patterns. After the artwork has dried, it is either left as is or coated with white sand from salty marshlands. *Lippan kaam* often adorns the walls of village homes and temples, as well as lobby areas.

Inspiration: The use of mirrors creates dazzling displays of light when *lippan kaam* is used in any area with natural or artificial lighting, making it the centre of attention in daytime as well as nighttime. Its intricate patterns and the contrast of the shimmering mirrors with the earthy tones of the clay also create a strong aesthetic impact.

Sustainability: The basic materials are organic and eco-friendly clay and camel dung. The mirrored pieces can be obtained from discarded material as well, allowing for reuse. The cooling properties of clay provide resistance to heat, making this an ideal form of cladding for exterior and interior walls, especially in hotter climates. Further, the use of *lippan kaam* also helps provide sustenance to artisan communities and keep a centuries-old craft alive. ■

Material: Clay, camel dung, mirror/glass pieces
Technique: *Lippan kaam*
Source Region: Gujarat, India
Studio: Manish Kumat Design Studio

Surface Decoration • 165

Surface Decoration

This restaurant features extensive hand-painted surface elements, which pay homage to Bengali art and culture. From the architectural features inspired by the artist Lalu Prasad Shaw, to the *pattachitra* art of Midnapore, this dining experience was meant to evoke the rich heritage of Bengal. As one enters the first floor, the huge wall, framed by a series of arches, displays traditional wall painting. The central hall provides a symbolic representation of a balcony on one side.

The smaller rooms house "Sara" paintings on the walls. These are augmented by wooden louvred fenestrations that allow filtered sunlight to enliven the interior.

Inspiration: The various arts of the Bengal region provided the primary inspiration for this mansion-turned-restaurant, to synchronize the dining experience with the rich cultural heritage of Bengal. Conceived in totality, it is expressed at different scales, from the architectural façade rendition to the design of light fixtures and window shutters.

Sustainability: This project demonstrates how the various artistic traditions of Bengal can be employed to create the design DNA of a space, thereby articulating the versatility of traditional arts and crafts, in addition to providing employment to craftspeople. ∎

Material: Custom-made paints
Technique: *Pattachitra* painting, illustrations, woodworking
Craftsperson(s): Mamoni Chitrakar (*pattachitra*)
Source Region: West Bengal, India
Studio: Abin Design Studio

Surface Decoration • 167

Surface Decoration

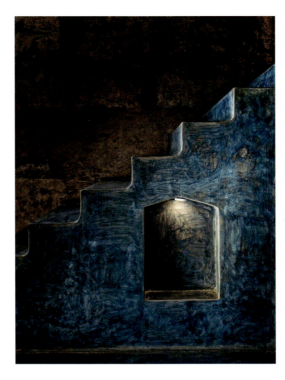

Ghutai is a form of traditional plastering. Interpreted as a monolithic handmade fabric, it tends to generate beautiful crack patterns, but necessitates the use of *kattai* (divisions). These dividers, when interpreted as inlay elements, enhance its explorative and creative value. Mixed on site with simple hand tools, the traditional components of *ghutai* are applied layer by layer and smoothened with a *gurumala* to conceal the inlay in the process. As they are sanded smooth, the hidden patterns reveal themselves, harmonizing with the colours that now come alive.

Inspiration: Challenging the current notion about manufactured goods being the best makes it crucial to understand and explore the possibilities in indigenous handmade techniques. Unlike the modernist modular that breaks the flowing space, *ghutai* offers a design solution extending from the floors to the walls, binding a space in itself. Moreover, the seamless stretch of *ghutai*, though simple, creates endless possibilities for texture, pattern, colour, infill and inlay, allowing for great customization.

Sustainability: This project involved a process of revival of art, innovated in today's time to continue a community and support their crafts instead of using factory-produced goods. Being an on-site job, it also minimized the efforts to cut, process and transport the materials, thereby greatly reducing waste. ■

Material: Cement oxides or chips, dolomite powder, *hirda* water, egg whites, water
Technique: *Ghutai, kattai*
Craftsperson(s): Bhagwandas Prajapati
Source Region: Maharashtra, India
Studio: PMA Madhushala

Surface Decoration • 169

Surface Decoration

China mosaic is the craft of embellishing surfaces through a composition of pieces of ceramic tiles, stones or glass mosaics. It can be used as internal or external flooring, wall surface decoration or on objects. The pieces can be cut by hand (with small tools or hammers) or by machines and laid out on mortar. Colourful compositions can be created by mixing pieces of different materials and forming patterns using stencils.

Inspiration: The craft is inspired from the traditional patterns seen on the terraces and floors of numerous old houses and *haveli*s. Further, given its flexibility in size, this craft offers fluidity and umpteen possibilities in patterns, which have been contemporized to create new and innovative designs for flooring and surface decoration.

Sustainability: The materials used for the craft can be second- or third-grade discarded ceramic tiles, cups and saucers, broken glass and stone pieces, which are recycled to form desired patterns. The surface helps to reflect light and reduce heat gain on terraces and gives a new dimension to interior spaces by bringing in nature in the form of light and beautiful patterns. ■

Material: Ceramic
Technique: Ceramic tilework
Craftsperson(s): Ashokbhai
Source Region: Gujarat and Rajasthan, India
Studio: Abhikram Architects, Panika Crafts and Technologies

Surface Decoration • 171

Surface Decoration

Gandhi nu Gam, at Ludiya in Kutch, was one of the 16 villages where Vastu Shilpa Foundation was involved with the rehabilitation processes after the 2001 earthquake. The inhabitants built their own traditional dwellings, called *bhunga*s, and undertook their ornamentation and decoration. Locally sourced Banni mud was used, along with cow dung and plaster, to create the surface finish, and then relief work was done with colours, patterns and mirrors to create an embroidered, embellished surface.

Inspiration: The ornamentation on the inside and outside walls is traditional, and its use of mud makes for a cool interior in the desert. The use of mirrors also helps brighten the surfaces in an otherwise dreary desert landscape.

Sustainability: All the materials were locally sourced and the inhabitants of the houses built the dwellings themselves. Also, in addition to providing employment and dignity after the earthquake, participation in this project ensured that traditional know-how was preserved and passed on to the next generation. It has also transformed this village into a tourist hub, creating further economic incentives. ■

Material: Banni mud, mirrors
Technique: *Lippan kaam*
Source Region: Gujarat, India
Studio: Vastu Shilpa Foundation

Surface Decoration

Traditionally painted murals can be found in many parts of India. In this project for a safari lodge, various methods of mural painting were applied contextually for maximum impact. The bathroom of the safari lodge featured wall paintings of animals in the Gond style, while the bar featured traditional gold leaf painting.

Inspiration: The safari lodge was situated in an area of abundant flora and fauna. The bar was luxurious and a place to relax and socialize, and hence the gold leaf painting.

Sustainability: Murals last for a very long time and use mostly organic pigments. In fact, over time, a mural gains more character with the formation of a patina. Murals are also a sustainable way to add glamour to a not-so-interesting interior element or surface while also having a very low carbon footprint. ■

Material: Natural pigments, gold leaf
Technique: Gond and Madhubani painting, gold leaf painting
Source Region: Central and northern India
Studio: Pradeep Sachdeva Design Associates

Surface Decoration

Madhubani is a very delicate and intricate style of painting from Mithila in eastern India. It requires highly skilled painters who draw the outlines and fill them in by hand. A variety of natural tools are used, such as twigs, brushes, matchsticks, as well as plant-based natural pigments.

Inspiration: The colours used in Madhubani art are vibrant and bold and usually depict themes drawn from nature and mythology. As the colours play an important role in depicting the mood of the painting, we felt the colours would reflect the mood of the interiors through this art form.

Sustainability: The colours used are all derived fully from plants and flowers and other organic materials. The implements used for painting are also nature-based, such as twigs and brushes made of wood and animal hair. Materials are locally sourced, and thus this wonderful art form is kept alive in a contemporary setting. ■

Material: Natural pigments, twigs, brushes
Technique: Madhubani painting
Source Region: Bihar, India
Studio: Manish Kumat Design Studio

Surface Decoration

The ancient art of Cheriyal painting inspired these products, giving a functional and utilitarian form to this type of scroll painting. A mixture of *shuddha matti* (white mud), rice starch, boiled tamarind seed paste and natural tree gum is mixed in proportion and is made into a slurry. It is evenly applied with bare hands on *khadi* cotton cloth. After the application of three coats on the cloth, it is allowed to dry naturally. Then the Cheriyal painting artist begins painting the scene, first adding an outline. Attractive borders are added at the end. In the contemporary usage here, a final Cheriyal scroll is fixed on the wooden log, which is then treated with garnish.

Inspiration: The essential idea was to create a subtle accent for interiors with hues of Indian-ness to fit across diverse, contemporary interiors. In its transformational form, the additional technique gives flexibility to create modern installations.

Sustainability: Tamarind seeds are aplenty in Telangana. Moreover, tamarind seeds and sawdust are biodegradable and work as natural hardeners. The carbon footprint of this product is very low as compared to other such products. It also helps in the revival of the craft tradition. ■

Material: Mud, rice starch, boiled tamarind seed paste, tree gum, other paints
Technique: Cheriyal painting
Craftsperson(s): D. Saikiran, Hyderabad
Source Region: Telangana and Andhra Pradesh, India
Studio: Xception the Design Studio

METAL

Old Core Gleams Once More

METAL

Old Core Gleams Once More

• Ayush Kasliwal

Other than gold, metal is rarely ever found in its native form in nature. Perhaps this is why gold has been one of the most enduring metals. Metal extraction from ores symbolizes a gigantic leap for human civilization. The Bronze Age, followed by the Iron Age, has had a lasting impact on almost every aspect of life, from shaping stone, to hunting and cooking.

The secrets of metal extraction had always been guarded zealously and, in many cases, were the cornerstones of entire economies. India in its heyday was at the cutting edge of metal extraction and had some of the finest metalworking skills in the world. This is proven by evidence of zinc mining and extraction in Zawar, Rajasthan, from as long ago as the 13th century CE, with many records indicating that India was one of the leading centres of metallurgy in the pre-industrial era.

This mastery over metallurgy is clearly indicated in the iron columns in modern-day Mehrauli, which, despite dating to the fifth century and containing 99 per cent iron in their composition, still stand rust-free today.

Sadly, documentation of these ancient skills of metallurgy is scarce and scattered, with an occasional specimen indicating the brilliance of Indian metalworking. The greatest achievements of Indian metalwork lie in the realm of jewellery, with impossibly fine work, masterful both in design and the virtuosity of construction. However, for the purpose of this essay, we will leave that aside, as it pertains more to personal adornment than to interior spaces.

There are craftspeople across the Indian subcontinent who use metal and express their skills using the material, not only as the primary material in their product, but also in tools that are essential for other crafts—for example, the making of blocks for printing, where the tools are made of metal, or through stone carving. Metal has also been used in the form of *vark,* or foil (used in paintings, *unani* medicine and to garnish Indian gourmet foods); as *zardozi* in embroidery, and in wires wrapped around yarn, used to weave the *zari* in saris. Here again, we will keep aside the vast arena of the making of tools, components and machines, and concentrate on crafts whose end products

PREVIOUS PAGES
A detail from a Bastar metal craft panel.
Image credit: Studio Lotus

RIGHT
A traditional *urli* from southern India, often used to prepare quick-cooling sweet dishes.
Image credit: Mapin

are primarily metallic objects. Everyday crafts, like those practised by the Gadia *lohar*s (the itinerant iron smiths going from village to village, repairing and retailing objects of daily use) or the *thathera*s (the utensil makers, who formed an essential part of any marketplace, rural or urban) or the incredibly skilled *sthapati*s (who mastered the art of bronze idol making) indicate the extensive spread of the metal craftsperson, encompassing the entire country.

For the sake of structure, we can broadly classify metal crafts into the following categories (which may be used on their own, or in combination, for the craftsperson is rarely one to limit themselves to a single method).
- Casting: The forming of metal by pouring liquid metal into cavities. The creation of the cavities can be done in several ways, and is often used to define the specific casting type.
- Sheet work, which includes:
  1. Forming: Hammering, folding, pressing or spinning metals through mechanical or manual means.
  2. Forging: This is the shaping of metal, typically when heated, by repeated hammering.
  3. Weaving: The weaving or making of meshes using strips or wires of metal.

Furthermore, there are various techniques of embellishment that can be performed on a cast or sheet-made object, such as:
- Inlay: The embedding of metal in wire or sheet form into or onto another metal object.
- Engraving: The creation of patterns or designs on metal using sharp tools to engrave patterns on the surface.
- Repoussé/chasing: The forming of metal sheets into patterns and designs by shaping them from the reverse or the front side.

This structure, detailed above, will be used in this essay to broadly introduce the various places in India where a particular technique is the dominant way of creating the product or is, at least, the one that it is most known for.

Casting

Casting is one of the oldest methods of forming metal—primarily because most methods of metal extraction yield liquid metal. It is a craft practised across different regions in the country—at an art and craft level, as well as at the industrial level. The famous statue of the dancing girl, from the Indus Valley Civilization, is a fine example.

There are numerous casting techniques, broadly classified into lost-wax casting, investment casting and sand casting. The lost-wax casting technique typically needs a form made out of wax, which, after being packed in a clay or plaster mould, is heated to leave a highly detailed cavity. The liquid metal poured into this cavity cools down and is obtained by simply breaking the mould. The sand casting technique, on the other hand, involves a pattern made out of wood or metal, and is used to create an impression in a sand mould, which is then used to create a cavity. Both these techniques are used extensively, in various iterations.

The casting of idols in Swami Malai, in Tamil Nadu, as well as the massive bell metal cooking vessels (called *urli*s), made by the Moosaris in Kerala, are highly refined crafts that use the lost-wax casting technique as a primary process. The making of the wax patterns and the

Gold foil is carefully pasted on a Thanjavur painting, in Tamil Nadu. Image credit: Mapin

Metal • 179

sciences and aesthetics behind them are both fascinating and beautiful, displaying a technical virtuosity. Subsequent to the casting, the idols are intricately chiselled and engraved to achieve an astonishing level of detail. Idols made in a lot of other places are typically sand-casted and are subsequently worked on to achieve great detail.

The metal mirrors from Aranmula are, likewise, another testimony to the incredible metallurgical skills of the country. These mirrors were once a household item, before the advent of the silver-backed glass ones that we see today, seen in statues in Sanchi and paintings in the Ajanta Caves. The mirrors are themselves made using an alloy of copper and tin and are framed in a sand-casted brass frame.

Another very common application of the casting process, especially in southern India, is that of making oil lamps and temple bells. While the oil lamps can be made in many different metals, the bells are made in a specific metal alloy called *kansa*, or bell metal, an alloy of copper with a high tin content. *Kansa* is also a material that is commonly used for utensils, primarily because it is sturdier and not as corrosive as brass. It is a difficult metal to work with as it has to be formed when it is still hot; however, casting is a relatively easy process and this is done widely across the country.

Udupi, in Karnataka, is another big centre for cast metal objects, both for daily-use objects (such as vessels and utensils) and for cast *bhoota* masks, used primarily for ritualistic purposes. Further north, *bidri* artisans from the town of Bidar use cast zinc shapes, which are adorned with silver, gold or copper wires, to create intricate objects.

Another widespread craft that uses casting is the *dhokra* technique. This is also a lost-wax process, in which beeswax is used in

A metal craftsman gives the final touches to a bronze idol of Swami Shanmugha, in Tamil Nadu.
Image credit: Mapin

An ornately carved wooden door, in Kerala, with intricate metal plating and handles in shape of peacocks.
Image credit: Dastkari Haat Samiti

the coiling process to create the shapes. This craft is practised widely across several states, primarily the ones with large tribal populations: Jharkhand, Odisha, West Bengal and Chhattisgarh, to name a few. One can easily spot a cast *dhokra* object with the telltale lines that are visible on its surface. While it appears to be a low-tech craft, it is an incredibly refined one and is unique to the subcontinent.

A very typical casted craft, practised in Jalesar, in District Etah in Uttar Pradesh, is that of casting *ghungroo*s (anklet bells), as used and seen popularly in Indian dance.

The cities of Moradabad, Aligarh, Hathras and Jalesar are known for their metalwork. All kinds of metal crafts are practised here, and Moradabad, especially, has come to be known across the globe. Though commonly not perceived as a traditional craft form, many of the metalworkers have been practising their craft for generations and have been able to refine it to meet not only global demands but also competitive price points.

While one may not immediately realize the extensive use of cast metal in interior spaces, it really is pervasive as a craft form and also as a method that is used widely, from hardware in doors and windows to plumbing fixtures. The ability of metal to take on just about any form opens up a host of possibilities. Added to this, the fact that it is commonly practised makes it a low-hanging fruit for designers to work with as a medium for interior product development. One need not always look for a well-known craft cluster: upon going to any auto repair shop or a utensil shop (preferably one that has been there for a long period of time) and asking, they might be able to find people to develop a product that is both unique and satisfying to the designer.

Sheet Work

Before the advent of the metal foundries and the industrial production of sheet metal, most sheets were hand-pounded from a soft alloy of metal. Making sheets is an incredible craft, not only on account of the skill that is needed but also because of the metallurgical knowledge needed to create soft malleable alloys. Although not practised extensively nowadays, there are many ways in which sheet metal is manipulated to create objects and surfaces. This also is a widely practised craft across most Indian states, typically in the form of utensils, the most common being the iron *tawa*, or the flat pan on which *rotis* are cooked. Like casting, this craft is carried out on a vast variety of scales: it is made on an industrial scale, as well as in small workshops by traditional craftspeople.

The malleability of metals allows one to bend and shape the sheets, which is why one can make incredibly complex shapes using metal, especially given the ability to weld these sheets together.

The easiest way to form metal is to beat it in a radial pattern over a metallic ring till it takes on a bowl-like shape. This craft is practised by a wide variety of people, typically called *thathera*s or *tamta*s, in northern India, who make common vessels and the occasional grand temple spire. (When passing through the areas where they work, there is an unmistakable sound of the wooden hammer hitting the metal.) This skill can be applied to make radially symmetrical objects and can be modified fairly easily into asymmetric shapes. The same craftspeople are adept at folding the metal as well as welding it. Interestingly, the welding is done using a traditional process that utilizes flux (in the form of *suhaaga*, or borax), which does not require either electric or gas-powered welding machines. One can find many examples of this craft in any local utensil store, where such vessels are preferred for ritualistic as well as aesthetic purposes.

Spires are perhaps the most common architectural application of this craft, and skilled craftspeople in Delhi, Jaipur and Lucknow can be seen making spires for monuments around the world.

Another process that is used to shape sheet metal is spinning. While not a traditional process, it is one of the most common ways of processing sheet metal. This process involves the compression of a sheet on a form while being spun on a lathe, such that it takes its shape. This almost always yields radially symmetric shapes and can be identified by tool lines that form around the spun object. Objects made using this technique are fairly common, and Moradabad is a massive centre for work of this kind. This method has been growing in use among a lot of traditional artisans, due to it being a faster method of production.

Stamping is also a technique that is used extensively. Large stampings are typically done industrially, owing to the requirement of large machines. There is a significant application of this process, especially for creating impressions on thin sheets, which are thereafter used as cladding material on furniture—a craft practised in Nathdwara and Udaipur, in Rajasthan.

There are many crafts that, while using sheets, do not fall in any of the categories mentioned above. For example, the flexible brass fish made in District Ganjam, in Odisha, are made by cutting and folding sheets that are linked to each other with a fine brass chain.

There are many other ways in which this craft is expressed using embellishment techniques, such as repoussé and chasing. Repoussé is typically done on the reverse of a metal sheet to create shapes and forms, or with the sheet fixed on a firm but malleable base, such as lac (a resin-like natural material). Chasing is a technique done on the front of the sheet. Both these techniques are used extensively in the making of objects of daily utility—for example, the *taashnari* (water jug) used in Kashmir or the architectural hardware from Ladakh. This technique is also used extensively to form the softer silver metal to make objects of utility, of practice of a faith, or just objects of beauty.

Along with repoussé and chasing, fretwork (using a fret saw) and chisel work are also used to cut through the metal to create delicate lace-like surfaces. Nokha, Nathdwara and Udaipur (in Rajasthan), Lucknow and Benaras (in Uttar Pradesh), Bhubaneshwar (in Odisha), Madurai (in Tamil Nadu) and Mysore (in Karnataka) are some of the well-known centres that practise this craft.

A hanging bell-metal lamp in Kerala.
Image credit: Dastkari Haat Samiti

Enamelling, or *meenakaari* work, has been historically used in jewellery but has also, of late, been used in embellishing many other metallic surfaces. Enamelling is the fusion of a vitreous material onto a metal. When applied on the whole surface, it is called *taam-chini* and is a technique done industrially. *Meenakari*, however, can be done on parts of a metal, leaving it partly exposed and partly covered. Decorative objects made in silver are enamelled in delicate jewel-like shades in Benaras. Contemporary enamel is practised in various parts of Maharashtra and in Delhi.

Forging, as a process, is commonly seen in rural areas, where the local ironsmith forges implements, farm tools and kitchen accessories. The Gadia *lohar* community is a nomadic community that goes from village to village (in Rajasthan, all the way to Andhra Pradesh) in fantastically decorated bullock carts and sets up shop beneath shady trees. Typically starting with metal billets, a skilled artisan is able to form it into any imaginable shape and form. The artisans of Bastar have refined this craft and now make animals, screens and a host of other objects. This craft has historically been used to make hinges and other architectural hardware, as well as weapons.

The Bandukiya community used to make traditional locks, with springs and secret keys, along with guns (now outlawed), while the Lohars, in Udaipur, still make fantastically decorated daggers with detailed metalwork—in a technique they call *koftgari*. These are also some of the few remaining communities that still know the technique of damascening, or watered steel, a technique that produces an especially strong and hard sword.

Wire Work
The village of Sultana, in District Jhunjhunu in Rajasthan, was known for its birdcages, which were made using recycled strips of metal sheets. They innovated on the craft and started making large shapes, which were made by coiling and interlacing wires on a welded inner armature. It has now become a popular craft and is carried out in several villages in Rajasthan, as well as in Moradabad.

The *tarkashi* (filigree) work of Odisha is done by welding thin strips of silver into delicate lace-like surfaces, which are then used to make a host of decorative items. This is a specialty of Odisha and is seen in both Cuttack and Puri. It can also be seen in a lot of other cities, albeit sporadically, as many of the metalworkers in jewellery-making workshops are from West Bengal and Odisha, and this craft has migrated across the country with them. •

Metal

 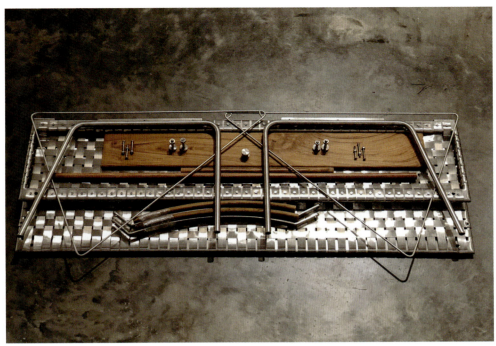

The craft of weaving can be traced back to 6000 BCE. The swing, too, as a piece of furniture, has a beautiful history, being mentioned in the Vastu Shastra as well. Over the centuries, swings have been made out of many materials. The manufacture of these swings uses the process of weaving with two components, warp and weft. Although metal is a hard material to weave, hand weaving was chosen for this project to get an essence of handicraft, passing it through a multistep process—cutting, threading, drilling, buffing and weaving—to create the breathable mesh. Various combinations of metals can be customized, and the addition of a patina (through oxidation) can provide a range of colours and textures.

Inspiration: Weaving renders strength and breathability to the material, making it very versatile, lightweight, and long-lasting. It also makes the surface flexible, providing comfort without any additional cushioning, with unmatched aesthetics.

Sustainability: Metal can be recycled and upcycled endlessly and flawlessly without any worries about product degradation. All metals such as stainless steel, brass and copper can be fully recycled and are valuable. The flatpack design also minimizes carbon footprint. ■

Material: Metal
Technique: Weaving
Craftsperson(s): Mahendrasinh Manubhai Gohil
Source Region: Gujarat, India
Studio: Rachaita Creative Solutions

Metal

Metal of various kinds has been used through the various spaces in the office, including but not limited to bell metal, copper and aluminium. The bell metal domes at the entrance contain 99 per cent copper and have been created in various sizes. Processed copper in two forms of patina, red and blue, has been used to create conference spaces and a free-standing wall within the office spaces on the fourth floor. The red patina is used in the conference room as vertical finishes and the blue patina has been used on the walls of the office.

Inspiration: The initial name for the building was the "Alchemist's Abode"—a reference to the patron's line of work. It was important that an allusion to this be made in the making of the space. To do this, we worked with various metals, processing them carefully to achieve various forms and colours—and hence the required results. Bell metal—normally processed to create bells for specific purposes—has been used to create

domes at the entrance of the building, which by the craftsmen's own admission is the first time that they have been employed in expressing the material in such a large and different form.

Sustainability: The crafts and techniques employed in these works move away from their traditional context both in terms of scale and method of use. The craft of bell metal casting has been optimized for functionality. The processed copper, in hues of red, blue and green, has been treated by proprietary processes using a range of salts and heat. On the whole, these present a wholly modern aesthetic, using the inherently traditional hand skills of the craftspeople employed. ■

Material: Metal
Technique: Bell metal casting and copper processing
Craftsperson(s): Yunus Luhar
Source Region: N.A.
Studio: M/s. Prabhakar B. Bhagwat

Metal

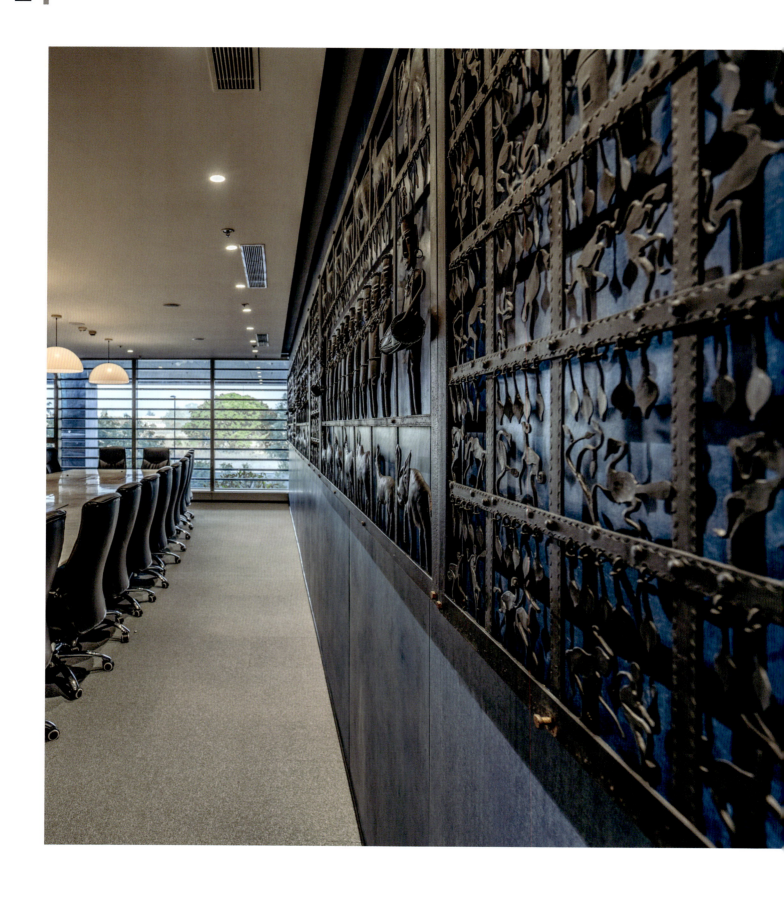

Trilegal's new offices formed the canvas for a series of vibrant Indian art and craft forms, executed in collaboration with artisans from Dastkari Haat Samiti. The boardroom employs a metal installation on the wall, featuring Chhattisgarh's famed Bastar metal craft. Depicting the cultural practices, musical instruments and fauna of the region, three metal panels handcrafted by Tiju Ram Vishwakarma complement the blue cement board walls. Scrap iron was beaten repeatedly at specific spots at a high temperature to attain the desired shape. Sharp edges and unnecessary portions were filed and smoothened, and, upon completion, varnish was applied to give the work a fine lustre. Its colour, derived from Trilegal's logo, adds a cool tonality to the space while creating a textured canvas for the craft to stand out.

Inspiration: This design was inspired by the desire to capture India's many craft traditions to create a distinct spatial identity for every zone or space in the office.

Sustainability: Scrap iron, which was sourced from Chhattisgarh for these pieces, can be recycled and given a second life. ■

Material: Scrap metal
Technique: Dhokra, or lost-wax metal casting
Craftsperson(s): Tiju Ram Vishwakarma
Source Region: Chhattisgarh, India
Studio: Studio Lotus, in collaboration with Dastkari Haat Samiti

Metal

India's age-old traditional metal craft, in particular the shape of a *tambal* or *kalash*, inspired this project, giving us a chance to work with coppersmiths in new, innovative design solutions.

1. Metal spinning: This is a process by which a sheet metal of 16 mm gauge is wrapped around and rotated by hand or a lathe machine. It is basically moulding a sheet metal over a dye. The collapsible dyes are made of acacia wood and metal is wrapped over it.
2. Firing process: Once the metal object is shaped, it is fired and put in an acid wash to strengthen the metal and then dipped in water to cool it.
3. Polishing, embossing and buffing: The form is polished with tamarind paste or lime and then embossed and buffed.

Inspiration: This project was based in humid Kerala, and we felt the corrosion-resistant properties of brass would be suitable for the climatic conditions there. Moreover, brass is very malleable and ductile. The metal craft traditions of Munnar in Kerala also provided several aspects of inspiration and reference.

Sustainability: This project already relied on the recycling of the scrap brass and copper without diminishing their composition, making it more energy-efficient compared to other metals. Not only does this make it cheaper but its corrosion-resistant properties also make it endure for a long time. ∎

Material: Metal
Technique: Metal spinning, firing, polishing, embossing and buffing
Craftperson(s): Balchandra Kadu
Source Region: Maharashtra and Kerala, India
Studio: Studio Earthworks

Metal

Sanjhi is a traditional form of stencilled paper-cutting that features exquisite designs and intricate picture motifs, cut into paper by a special small scissor. Here, the cutwork pattern was transferred onto plywood after removing the cutouts. The remaining plywood was covered in antique-finish bronze foil and used as a backdrop for seating in the living area. The same panel was later resized, covered with silver foil and reused for the client's new house as a back-panel for the bed.

Inspiration: From an original *sanjhi* papercut of the "Tree of life." ■

Material: Plywood, bronze foil, silver foil
Technique: Inspired by the traditional paper-cutting technique of *sanjhi*
Craftsperson(s): Artisans under the supervision of Alok Paliwal
Source Region: Uttar Pradesh, India
Studio: S+PS Architects

Metal

Sanjhi is a traditional paper stencilling craft of cutting intricate designs into paper with a special small scissor. Here, inspiration was taken from the motifs of this craft, as well as similar enclosures in old buildings in Fort, Mumbai, to create an open-mesh installation around an elevator. In keeping with the client's devotion to Lord Krishna, a vertical Vrindavan Garden, which climbed up three storeys, was conceptualized. The original motifs were adapted and transformed digitally, by drawing and revising them to suit the fabrication process. Finally, these were woven by hand by artisans at a workshop in Bengaluru, facilitated by an Indo-Dutch collaboration called Lace Fence.

Inspiration: The house where this open-mesh enclosure was installed is called "Kanha," as the family residing there are steeped in the ethos of Lord Krishna. The driving idea behind this project was a desire to combine the family's devotion to Lord Krishna with the aesthetics of certain older buildings in Fort. In other words, how could we combine something Indian with something industrial?

Sustainability: Instead of a closed lift cage with the use of lots of material and artificial light, this was a naturally lit and ventilated elevator shaft. In both this and the project on the facing page, there is a strong element of social sustainability, which keeps these crafts alive and provides livelihoods to artisan communities. ■

Material: Mild steel box section outer frame with metal-mesh weaving
Technique: Metalwork inspired by the traditional paper-cutting technique of *sanjhi*
Craftsperson(s): Lace Fence, Karnataka
Source Region: Uttar Pradesh, India
Studio: S+PS Architects

Metal • 193

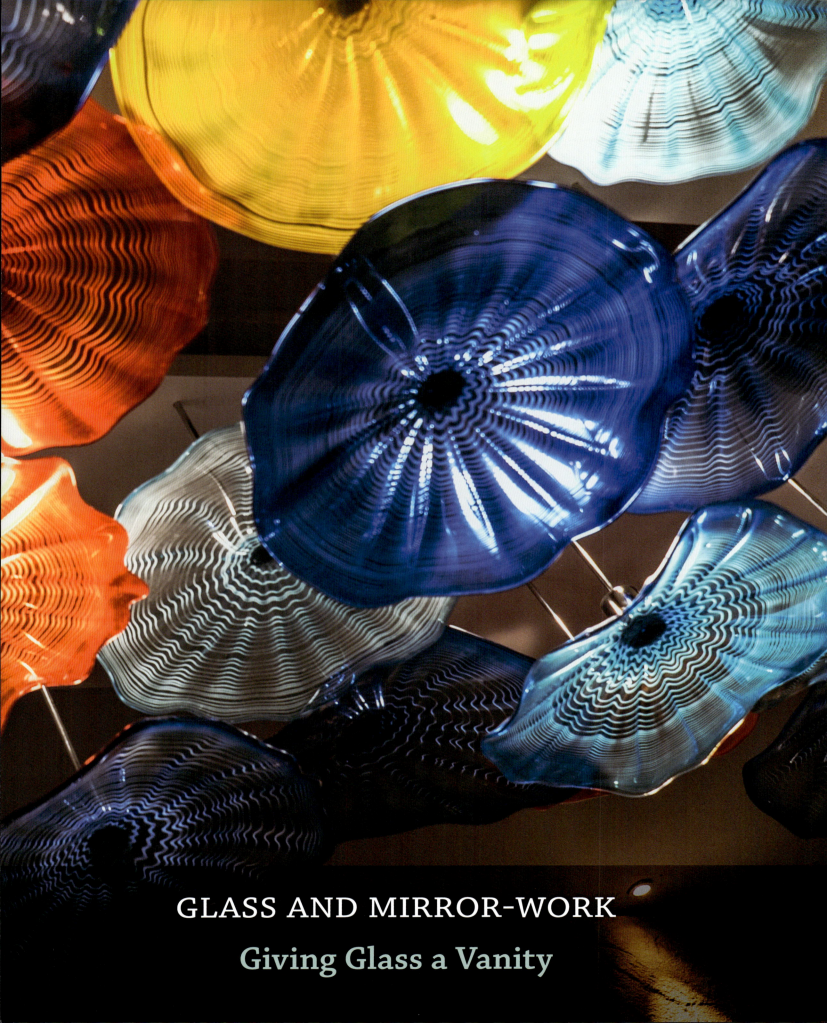

GLASS AND MIRROR-WORK

Giving Glass a Vanity

GLASS AND MIRROR-WORK

Giving Glass a Vanity

• Arjun Rathi and Jaya Jaitly

The crafting of glass in architecture and embellishment, when compared to the more recent creation of utility objects such as vases or tableware, has a much older history. Perhaps it all began with the use of mica shards found in sandy soil, which attracted nomadic communities across central Asia to use small pieces to add shine to their clothing and jewellery. This was the origin of embroidering them into women's clothing and the ornamentation of cattle and horses. They reflected the sun and resembled gold and silver. Inside living structures made of clay, they were embedded into the walls. If a

lamp were lit inside this hut, it would result in the entire space reflecting tiny shimmers of light, creating a magical effect. These nomadic tribes travelled and later settled across many countries, including India. Communities using glass embellishment are still very much in existence in Rajasthan, Gujarat, Maharashtra, Andhra Pradesh and Karnataka. In Kutch, Gujarat, the embedding of glass in walls with both mud and cement surfaces is now not just a personal choice but a tourist attraction. The great favourites of royalty, glass mirrors of all sizes were used in abundance on the walls and ceilings of their palaces. The City Palace in

PREVIOUS PAGES
Blown-glass lighting designs at The Lodhi Hotel, inspired by the colours of an Italian spring.
Image credit: Arjun Rathi Design

RIGHT
A stained-glass panel inside the St. Thomas Cathedral in Mumbai.
Image credit: iStock

FACING PAGE
The tradition of stained-glass painting is applied here to create a beautiful panel depicting Krishna and his gopis.
Image credit: iStock

Udaipur, the Sheesh Mahal in Dungarpur, Aina Mahal in Kutch, and the Chandra Mahal in the City Palace in Jaipur are grand architectural displays of pomp and splendour. *Aina* or *shisha*, local terms for mirrors, always added that extra magic to any form of architecture, from tiny mud huts to the splendid dwellings of kings.

There have been several craft skills using glass in India, starting around 1000 BCE with the prolific manufacture of glass beads for local and export markets because of the abundant availability of quartz materials such as chalcedony, agate, onyx, jasper and rock crystal.

Mosaic lamps of different-coloured glass pieces are made in Jaipur even today. Mirror frames in a particular type of craftsmanship, in which glass pieces are embedded into clay, cement or plaster of Paris, are unique to Udaipur. Millions of bangles and glass droplets for chandeliers and tiny, industrially cut mirror chips come from the famous glass town of Firozabad in Uttar Pradesh. In Bhuj, Kutch, in the 1980s, there was an old craftsman who painted images on the bottom half of small rectangular mirrors, with cheap aluminium sheets edging the mirrors like a tin frame. These were attached to the flaps of a *toran* hung on doorways to welcome visitors, in an act of embellishing a dwelling. He was the last of his clan and, sadly, the tradition did not get passed on to a younger generation, but his images often consisted of social comment about colonial rule, amidst floral borders or ornamental flower vases.

The technique of Tanjore painting involves painting on the reverse of glass, a technique practised by Sneh Gangal, a young artist in Delhi. She scrapes away portions of the silvering, by which a reflective substance is painted on glass to form a mirror, and paints from the reverse in the transparent areas. Finally, there is the unique craft of mirror making in the tiny town of Aranmula in Kerala. It is called Aranmula *kannadi* (mirror) but the material is an alloy of metals in a highly polished and burnished state, which is brought about by a technique that has remained a family secret for generations. Recently revived for a larger variety of designs and uses, it is a preciously retained skill that gives expensive materials the appearance of glass, a less expensive material, and that is what makes it unique.

In fact, glass is one of the most exciting and magical materials to experiment with. Sand, limestone and soda ash, in specific compositions, combine to create an often transparent material. Surprisingly, a lot of the raw materials used for

Glass and Mirror-work • 197

An ornate chandelier, using dozens of lamps and arrays of crystal or glass, is used as a decorative ceiling-mounted fixture at the Jama Masjid in Delhi. Image credit: iStock

glass are similar to those used to create cement, but both materials are diametrically opposite in properties, transparency and strength. This wonderful material is sustainable, endlessly recyclable and provides great environmental benefits. This means that glass can be used over and over; today's waste glass can be melted down, reshaped and repurposed as a new product tomorrow.

The uniqueness of glass starts with its own special way of transmitting light, becoming, as a result, the favourite material for architects and lighting designers. Even simple colours in the material appear very rich and vibrant, unique to glass due to its reflective properties.

The versatility of the material allows for a multitude of creative opportunities. Glass in its solid form is melted in a kiln, which allows it to set into a pre-defined mould. The kiln-casted glass process is popular among artists due to the ease of set-up and has extensive applications in cutlery, accessories, furniture design, lighting fixtures, and wall and frame panelling for interior design. As a studio, we use the process to create textured glass panels for interiors and thicker slabs for our range of cast-glass furniture and lighting. The studio's cast-glass collections take inspiration from the textures of frozen lakes, and use the kiln-casting process to create slabs of glass that mimic the texture of frozen ice.

Another popular form of shaping glass is glass blowing, a technique that has been in use since the first century BCE. The technique consists of inflating molten glass with a blowpipe to form a sort of glass bubble, which can be moulded into glassware for practical or artistic purposes. In the interiors and design industry, products from hand-blown glass are extensively used for décor, lighting, furniture and accessories. The mechanized version of this process, through mould blowing, allows for quick reproduction of designs where required. Due to the industrialized nature of the process, a majority of the glass industry has been set up in Firozabad, near Agra, in Uttar Pradesh.

The infrastructure for formal glass education is sporadically spread across the country, with a few universities offering a short course in glass-blowing and glass-casting techniques. Blown glass hasn't been the most accessible process due to the remote location of Firozabad and the absence of local studios in different areas of the country. This, overall, has kept indigenous

In these paintings, the artist Sneh Gangal transposes the Kangra miniature style onto a mirror, painting the images in reverse. For this series, she has depicted scenes from the Geet Govind, a celebrated love poem dedicated to Lord Krishna.
Image credit: Dastkari Haat Samiti

experimentation by designers low and has become a big opportunity for import markets to sell blown glass products and accessories.

To give better accessibility to blown glass techniques, we recently set up the Rural Modern Glass Studio in Chembur, Mumbai. It will be the first publicly accessible local blown glass studio, which will be open to designers and enthusiasts to come and experiment with hot-glass techniques, as well as to have public workshops and courses to encourage a new generation of glass artists. The glass studio will also look to up-skill Indian glass artisans through formal courses, which will allow our studio to explore the material in a more hands-on way for our lighting design and other experiments.

Our studio extensively uses the hand-blown glass process to create lighting installations for interior spaces: *The Italian Bloom*, at The Lodhi Hotel, New Delhi, created an art installation, 102 feet in length, of hand-blown glass flowers inspired by Italian spring colours.

One of our signature products, the Shikhara Hanging Pendant, takes inspiration from the five elements of Earth, Fire, Air, Water and Ether. It is composed of large blown glass forms combined with metal frames to create a collection of hanging pendants. The blown glass forms are produced in collaboration with the artisans of Firozabad, who are very skilled with mould-blowing techniques.

The *Blue Wave* lighting installation, which our studio designed for the World Towers, the tallest residential building in the world, located in Mumbai, consisted of 8,200 cast-glass elements, which had textures of flowing water. The installation was inspired by the waves in the sea, and involved hanging these cast-glass modules to create a ceiling-suspending lighting installation for the building's private banquet hall.

Industrially produced glass processes were experimented with, through our Bauhaus Collection, which combined sleek metal frames with industrially produced blown glass spheres in opaline glass. The round shape and shiny white colour of opaline glass used for the collection was inspired by pearls; in a fluid jewellery-like style, the pearls were combined with metal frames to create a mass-producible lighting collection. The glass again is industrially produced in Firozabad through a process of machine lathe blowing.

Due to the versatility and extensive application of glass, as a studio we are always passionately looking for new ways to use glass in our work. With the growing nature of the interiors and design industry in the country, glass as a material has stood the test of time and will always be in demand in growing markets. •

Glass and Mirror-work

Stained-glass artwork has been a part of church interiors and architecture since medieval times. The altar backdrop seen here features the cross, silhouetted by natural light, surrounded by a radiating illuminated glass installation. Warm-toned glass panes were cut and fitted into a custom-made M.S. framework. The windows in the church were fitted with coloured glass panes, which were etched with religious symbols and then fired in a kiln to emulate the qualities of traditional stained-glass panels found in churches all over the world.

Inspiration: Since stained-glass art has been seen in churches since medieval times, it made sense to reimagine it in a more contemporary form, both to ornament the space and to create a reverential atmosphere for the faithful. Hence, light had to be manipulated to create a spiritual atmosphere.

Interpretations of this craft, such as an illuminated glass installation, coloured panes with symbols and traditional imagery, were used to permeate the space with light and ensure the revival of a dying art.

Sustainability: The timelessness of the design and the eternal quality of stained glass will ensure that these installations stand the test of time. The stained-glass interventions will be sustainable in the long run as they will be ingrained in the fabric of the church and thus will be irreplaceable. ■

Material: Glass
Technique: Stained-glass artwork
Craftsperson(s): Swati Chandgadkar/The Glass Studio
Source Region: Maharashtra, India
Studio: Ainsley Lewis/Urban Interventions Studio

Glass and Mirror-work • 201

Glass and Mirror-work

Mirror-work has played a very important role in the traditional décor of Rajasthan and Gujarat. The art of *thikri*, or glass inlay, involves cutting pieces of blown glass by hand using diamond scalpels. These pieces are then arranged into the desired shapes and assembled on various surfaces, such as ceilings, walls or objects, to form stylized geometric patter

Inspiration: The use of this craft was inspired by certain vernacular settlements—which use mirrors embedded in mud—and palaces such as the Sheesh Mahal. Contemporary interpretations of this craft for modern spaces give a traditional touch and make us feel connected to our valuable heritage.

Sustainability: The small pieces of mirrors that are used in *thikri* work are recycled pieces of broken mirrors, which are then arranged to form beautiful traditional patterns. Such sustainable traditional artwork promotes local

artisans and their craft. Since most of the work is executed by local craftsmen headed by the master craftsman, the processes and the technologies rooted in their traditions are preferred. ∎

Material: Mirrors
Technique: *Thikri* work
Source Region: Rajasthan, India
Studio: Abhikram Architects, Panika Crafts and Technologies

Glass and Mirror-work • 203

Glass and Mirror-work

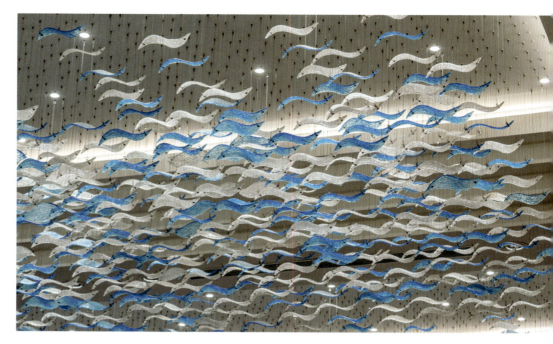

As a lighting design studio, most of our composite works and installations involve collaboration with various metal, glass and other craft artisans across the country. Combining traditional crafts with modern fabrication techniques and materials has been the core process for us to build our works. Since most of our products have different combinations of metal, glass and wood, the processes on each material vary. With regards to glass, the studio explores two forms of production processes: blown glass, blown either by hand or lathe machine, and casted glass, where raw glass is melted and shaped into slabs used for lighting or glass furniture.

Inspiration: Glass is an integral material for decorative lighting. It creates unique shadows when lit, and the material has the ability to give a very rich colour. Through our glass casting process, we are able to create a version of glass that looks like slabs of frozen ice and is very unique to the process.

Sustainability: Glass is an infinitely recyclable material. Waste glass can be melted down and reshaped into a new product. Moreover, our works use natural brass and copper for the frames, which are also recyclable. In terms of social sustainability, we work with artisans from Firozabad, in Agra, providing employment and skilling opportunities. We are also in the process of setting up a school in Mumbai where artisans can learn hot-glass techniques for glass blowing. ■

Material: Glass, metal
Technique: Glass blowing and casting
Source Region: Uttar Pradesh, India
Studio: Arjun Rathi Design

Glass and Mirror-work

The essence of India in Washington, D.C., Punjab Grill is a restaurant located very close to the White House. This fine-dining restaurant was designed and produced entirely using traditional Indian crafts. Everything—from the stone wall panels, veneer *jaali*s, furniture, brass *jaali*s, arches, brass-inlaid tiles of granite, the basin counter, the ornamental gold leaf mirror to the Indian marble inlay flooring—was handcrafted in Jaipur with local materials. Traditional techniques of *thathera* hand-hammered metalwork, *thikri* hand-cut mirror-work, stone carving and wood carving, and sand casting have been transported to a grand setting. The entire restaurant was built and assembled in India, dismantled and shipped in about five shipping containers and finally reassembled on site.

Inspiration: For the best Indian restaurant in Washington, D.C., the design had to be the epitome of Indian design sensibilities in a contemporary setting. Envisioned as a modern rendition of the Sheesh Mahal, or the Palace of Mirrors, the lustre and intricacy of brass, mirror-work, stone and wood carvings together bring out the magnificence and grandeur of the place.

Sustainability: All the materials used in this project were repurposed, long-lasting, handcrafted and natural. ■

Material: Stone, wood, glass, mirrors, metal
Technique: *Thathera* metalwork, *thikri* mirror-work, stone carving, wood carving, sand blasting
Craftsperson(s): Raghav (stone carving), Kishan (*thikri* mirror-work)
Source Region: Rajasthan, India
Studio: AnanTaya, AKFD

Glass and Mirror-work • 207

HERITAGE PROPERTIES

Old Stones Sing Again

HERITAGE PROPERTIES

Old Stones Sing Again

• Aman Nath

Rather than complain about the paths history inevitably forges—where some get acclaim and others get ruined—in whichever era we are born, we should consider ourselves fortunate to be alive in body and spirit. For me, the mid-20th century was a great era to observe where India and its crafts were placed and how we all slowly grew out of the spell of the "phoren-made" by the end of our adolescence.

But before that, to first understand how seriously all things indigenous were threatened or made extinct by India's colonization by the British, a look at history and some of the facts can be quite revealing. What began somewhat as a side-battle of Plassey, in 1757, between the Nawab of Bengal and his French allies in the defence of his lands against the British East India Company, was to become a scenario of greed and aggrandizement within a century. In 1858, India came to be directly administered by the British Crown. A whole process of Indian patronage becoming embarrassed or even ashamed of its tastes led to the blind emulation of European architecture, led by a few good architects but mainly engineers and draughtsmen who did not represent the best of their traditions. The Gothic married the Indo-Islamic to give birth to the Indo-Saracenic hybrid, best suited for railway stations and functional public buildings. In the process, many of our grand building traditions slipped away and were finally lost. Fortunately, the temples of India carried some of the craft patronage, but the toll on crafts used by individuals was immense.

If you think of the recent legacy that 565 royal houses and thousands of *zamindari* estates and *jagir*s, which comprised 40 per cent of pre-Independence India and 23 per cent of its population, left behind in the last three centuries, there is little of our artistry and tradition in the building crafts that have been carried forward. Very few residential buildings leave us proud of India. With the onslaught of tourism, many of the palaces and forts began to play out of the European model and use Indian fabrics and objects to attract discerning travellers. They didn't want to see or live out a repetition of their familiar styles. This bonus still persists, as more and more Heritage Hotels become showcases of India's best crafts.

A site on the Tentative List of UNESCO World Heritage Sites, the Padmanabhapuram Palace in Tamil Nadu (owned and maintained by the Government of Kerala), the first seat of the rulers of Travancore, predates the colonial period. Built between 1550 and 1750, it displays the most spectacular indigenous craft and building skills. Seven years before the decisive Battle of Plassey, the Palace intuitively shied away into itself, as if it had heard the death knell. With a plinth of the local coastal laterite stone, it is built entirely out of timber and clay. The Palace's 14 purposes of usage, which are now highlighted—the entrance porch and reception halls, on to the living quarters, dining hall and kitchen, spaces for rituals and prayers, the armoury, entertainment and dance halls, mansions, palaces—all make for stunning need-based spaces. The craftsmanship adorns where necessary, without any hint of excess or decadence.

A similar random but more modest example in the far north of India would be the Stok Palace at Leh, perched on a cliff of earthy mountains. Built completely by local artisans with a full understanding of extreme weather conditions, it uses the warmth of mud for its adaptability and wood for its flexibility to weather. Frescoes from 1820 onwards show no alien influences, with no

PREVIOUS PAGES
An aerial view of Tijara Fort-Palace, Rajasthan

inferiority complexes that harbour a compulsion to borrow from all those sea-faring nations who influenced our buildings to an irreversible degree, which now seem beyond repair. Danish architecture in Tranquebar, Portuguese in Calicut and Goa, French in Pondicherry (now called Puducherry) and Karikal, Dutch in Kochi, not to mention the British all over the subcontinent, intimidated India out of its building strength, possibly forever.

Where has that science of carpentry, once proudly called "taccusastra," gone today? Who will teach again the formulae, site selection, orientations, governing proportions, scale dimensions—in fact, the whole genetic code, which relates to the availability of timber lengths, their thickness and strength in relation to the needs of specific regions, the steeply sloping roofs related to the run-off rate of the rain, as well as the lower heat retention of terracotta tiles? When will our patrons and architects of today rise to the occasion to look deep within the vernacular traditions?

But we can still hark back to better days with hope for the future. In Kerala, where dexterity, skill and restraint are balanced in equal measure, or in Pondicherry, where the French brought some simplicity to the Tamil design excess, it is quite easy even today to restore or replicate the old. The new cannot be told from the old. In Kerala's wooden grilles, which screen off spaces but let the breeze pass, there is much to learn from and adapt. Throughout India, wood-working traditions are still found to be vibrant,

such as the *khatamband* tradition of intricately carved ceilings, which Shah-i-Hamadan had brought to Kashmir from Persia and which now continues to flourish in its mechanized form, whereby 2,000 pieces can be made in a day. Once a purely luxury item, *khatamband* ceilings are more widely used today. It is as if the geometric-patterned, marble-inlaid floors of the Mughals are now on the ceilings too!

From my own experience, in the course of the whole Neemrana adventure to revitalize some 30 properties in 18 states, it was thrilling to find Gyarsi Lalji of Jaipur, who had retired from the Maharaja Sayajirao University of Baroda after teaching the art of true *fresco buono* painting, or *avayish*, on wet lime plaster. We used this process for the dados and floors of the older wings at Neemrana Fort-Palace. It was amazing to see how lime was filtered three times and applied in layers and then burnished with an agate stone. In Pondicherry, we discovered that a similar finish was achieved by grinding seashells, applied with plaster of Paris and then polished with coconut oil.

I feel that if there is sufficient interest and research done, the passion to revive crafts bears fruit. Craftspeople in India can rejuvenate the lost skills of other building crafts also, which were not necessarily practised by their forefathers. With new, forward-looking generations, who are also keen to look back under the layers of the past, there is much hope in revivalism, into which the strengths of the 21st century can breathe new life. •

Heritage Properties

The Tijara Fort-Palace, an unfinished ruin from the 1830s, restored and revitalized by Aman Nath, is now literally a show window for the crafts of India and its creative people. The cool Surya Mahal at Tijara Fort-Palace is sparsely furnished to do justice in showcasing its *durrie* floor, laid out permanently. The suite uses only leftover materials and waste, like the chipped china plates attached to the inside of the dome. Painters skilled in the art of miniature painting were commissioned to paint mangoes on the china. In this suite designed by Surya and Ritu Singh, the floor is designed by Aman Nath. ■

Tijara Fort-Palace, Rajasthan
Studio: Neemrana/Aman Nath

Heritage Properties • 213

Heritage Properties

This craft visually transfers the patterns of the *durrie* weaves to iron moulds, which are then filled with coloured cement paste. The tiles are manually compressed in a press and then dried and cured under water. The effect is much the same as a large *durrie* spread in a Durbar hall—especially when it is dimly lit with candles or indirect lighting. The complexity of the tile manufacture complements the dexterity of the carpet weaving. Laid in the Mardana Durbar, they complement the exquisite detail of the pillars, which have every centimetre chiselled in such detail as if it was a bar of soap!

Inspiration: This design was inspired by the largest carpet loom in Bikaner Jail, which I saw while working on the book *Arts and Crafts of Rajasthan* (Mapin, 1994). These looms could turn out monumental masterpieces for India's Durbar halls. The challenges of maintaining such large *durrie*s—spreading them out, removing them when the seasons changed, sunning and dusting them, and filling the roll with dried neem leaves to protect them from insects and rodents—brought out the dilemma of using *durrie*s in dusty, open spaces. Not handwoven, but handcrafted, these were imagined like precious weaves permanently pressed under glass, as if preserved for posterity.

Sustainability: Much like the Italian *pietra dura*, the art of cutting coloured stones—even semi-precious ones—and inlaying them in other stones such as marble, almost without any gaps, renders floor tiles as permanent as the architecture where they are laid. Even the *fresco buono*, the Italian art of wall painting in natural pigments on wet-lime walls, made the art as permanent as the architecture it adorned. The two lived and died together as did the Roman mosaic floors, which remained preserved after millennia, as seen at Pompei, where volcanic ash had buried a whole city. ■

Tijara Fort-Palace, Rajasthan
Studio: Neemrana/Aman Nath

Heritage Properties • 215

Heritage Properties

This design, in the Laila Mahal, champions the elegant patchwork done by the women of Kutch under the guidance of Laila Tyabji, the *grande dame* of crafts in India, the founder of Dastkar, a leading Indian initiative to organize the best of the diverse craft talents. This gives them a forum to market their wares as also to upgrade designs, which help their crafts attain a contemporary appeal, wherever necessary. The Laila Mahal also features Khurja pottery from Uttar Pradesh and the specially commissioned Mata ni Pachhedi hand-painted textile from Gujarat, which hangs above the beds.

Inspiration: The whole journey of Laila Tyabji is an inspiration and an ode to the genius of India's craftspeople. Beginning in Gujarat, where she revitalized the crafts of the desert state, she has gone on to rekindle the creative fires of the crafts of almost all regions in India.

Sustainability: Indian crafts, which have survived so many centuries, have their inbuilt sustainability, until threatened by industrialization and indiscriminate urbanization. Many efforts by government bodies and passionate individuals have seen that Indian crafts survive this danger. The heritage hotels of India have played the role of *noblesse oblige* to showcase these crafts to the world and ensure their longevity. ∎

Tijara Fort-Palace, Rajasthan
Studio: Neemrana/Aman Nath

Heritage Properties • 217

Heritage Properties

The abandoned Sheesh Mahal of the Raja of Neemrana, which didn't compare with the more famous ones in the Mughal or Rajput capitals, had its own provincial whimsicality unique to itself. This had been vandalized over four decades and was home to cooing pigeons and their droppings. But a few remnants that had clutched on to the past were clues enough to recreate the whole gold-and-brown ceiling.

Inspiration: The inspiration to enhance and carry forward the past must come from the past. Remnants of the original blue-green tint on the walls and the replication of the gilded ceiling fragments recreated the ambience of the room. A white floor border suggested a *durrie*, which was woven to size but the challenges of its maintenance—in a dusty place with heavy colonial furniture on it—gave way to weaves that are inlaid into the tiles of the floor. All these elements combine to recreate the early 20th century, which receives guests in this room of the 15th-century Neemrana Fort-Palace.

Sustainability: The Neemrana Fort-Palace remains a foremost and iconic example of sustainability with a capital "S." The term "Neemranification" is synonymous with restoration, revitalization and interventions that contemporize old ruins so that they can become viable and forge their way into the future with a venerable reverence that will continue to maintain them. ∎

Neemrana Fort-Palace, Rajasthan
Studio: Neemrana/Aman Nath

Heritage Properties • 219

Heritage Properties

The Shiv Niwas renovation was a process of upgradation of the upper and lower level suites, palace rooms next to the Shiv Pol and the public areas. The public areas and 39 guest rooms, with different needs, themes and ambiences, were refurbished individually in context of their history.

Inspiration: The 75-year-old lotus paintings on the walls and ceilings of the Durbar hall, and its forms, colour palette and silver sofa chairs laid the foundation for the theme of the Imperial Lotus Suite. The fountain, furniture and fabrics in the suite were custom-made in close collaboration with craftspeople. Flooring was redone in white and pink Makrana marble, and a single stone fountain that resembled an open lotus with 12 petals, representing the 12 months of a year, was placed in the centre. The headboard of the Bed Pavilion, with entwining lotuses and leaves, was cast in white metal in Ahmedabad. The ceiling of the poster bed, a trellis of lotuses, was a fine example of hand-cut white metal sheet work, executed in Udaipur. Bed curtains were specially woven in translucent Maheshwari silk, strewn with small white lotuses. The rest of the bed surfaces and arches were made in wood, some carved and covered with pressed metal and some with embossed white metal. The lotus creeper design was embroidered by hand on the bed, while the cushion covers were screen-printed manually and the tassels handcrafted to suit the colour palette of the room.

Sustainability: The Palace Complex itself and its craftspeople comprised a large repository of knowledge of materials and techniques of construction/restoration. The involvement of these craftspeople, as well as that of textile designers, embroiderers and manufacturers of tassels, produced works that were far superior to customized machine-made products. ■

Shiv Niwas Palace, Rajasthan
Studio: Abhikram Architects

Heritage Properties • 221

Heritage Properties

Over a century old, the four-storeyed Fateh Prakash Palace overlooks Lake Pichola, forming a part of the Palace Complex. A large Durbar hall, or royal court, was located on the third floor. Its main arrival level was converted into a banquet hall. Its corridors, auxiliary spaces and meeting rooms, which were long ago converted into living quarters, were now converted into suites on the third and fourth floors. A restaurant next to the banquet hall (facing the lake) and a Crystal Gallery on the top floor were some other additions.

Inspiration: Every space and element had a story to tell about the materials and the evolution of their appropriate use over many centuries. The old furniture and electrical fixtures were restored and the original heritage chandeliers in the Durbar hall provided inspiration for the design of new crystal chandeliers. The paintings provided the basis for the colour palette and, overall, the pairing of furniture and electrical fixtures was done to balance the ambience of a traditional palace with contemporary needs.

Sustainability: The scale of the space and the calibre of detailing required led to the use of extremely simplified methods and mechanisms. Restoration and reuse of old furniture and electrical fixtures, and the local manufacture of new ones, helped cut down the costs to a large extent. ■

Fateh Prakash Palace, Rajasthan
Studio: Abhikram Architects

Heritage Properties

The House of MG is the first and largest adaptive reuse project in Ahmedabad, Gujarat. The ancestral family of the current owners have had a significant influence on the city and are acknowledged to have introduced India to architectural modernism, through Le Corbusier and Louis Kahn, whom they invited to design many of the city's premier institutions. This exposure ensured a contemporary yet cohesive approach in the design philosophy that relied on the family's strong cultural roots and Gandhian ideology, combined with a global outlook and sensibility. The emphasis was on using local materials, local talent and personal aesthetics that were honed over years of growing up in an environment that put huge emphasis on arts and culture. This stands out in an era of aspirational luxury and is evident in the authenticity of the outcome. The furniture and textiles are made locally, and the staff is hired from the city or from the neighbouring villages. The interior decoration is also formed along local themes, derived either from Islamic motifs seen in the (famous) mosque on the other side of the street or from Vaishnava religious art, such as the Mata ni Pachhedi tradition of hand-painted textiles. All aspects of the property tell a story, articulated on signboards for the benefit of guests. The intangible aspects of the adaptive reuse play a big role in highlighting the identity of the place as a former residence of a cultured Gujarati family. ■

The House of MG, Gujarat
Studio: House of MG

Heritage Properties

A Case Study

After obtaining his Bachelor's degree in Commerce, in Kolkata, Sunil Rampuria could have worked only on the bottom lines of his businesses, so that the next generation might move from a golden to a platinum spoon in their mouth. But when construction activity took him to the port town of Vishakhapatnam in 1983, it was the building of apartments that took a sidestep. On journeys to his hometown in the desert kingdom of Bikaner, he was fascinated by the lesser-known craft of *usta* work. In 1985, he began embellishing his large ancestral *haveli*, established by his industrialist-philanthropist grandfather, Dadosa Bhanwar Lal ji, which has 41 rooms over three storeys, built around a grand courtyard.

The *ustad*s, or master craftsmen, would stay in the *safaa* rooms on the ground floor, where turbans once bobbed their colours from the pegs. Rampuria, their patron, a latter-day Medici, would dash in and out of Bikaner for week-long stints. In 1992, Bhanwar Niwas, now gilded to a new finesse, opened to rave reviews. Crafts had married architecture in a new disguise and the heritage bride became the pride of Bikaner. But the art, craft and building bug had bitten deep into Rampuria, who was to come up with his own *pièce de résistance* in the Gaj Kesri Hotel in Bikaner.

The Gaj Kesri is all new but it evokes Rampuria's fine traditional sensibilities. Besides reviving and continuing the

specialized art of brickwork, the hotel uses broken-china mosaic on its floors—an art called *tukri* in Rajasthan and *kapchi* in Gujarat. It uses *usta* work in the border panels and dados, and spread across the property are other great sparks of design and craft that are famous in Rajasthan. ■

Gaj Kesri, Rajasthan
Studio: Sunil Rampuria

Taking miniature paintings to new heights are these 3D architectural models, which have been converted into wall art.

This beautiful, bespoke wall art is a fine example of *Usta* work, with gold leaf applied to the surface, by the brothers Iqbal Usta, Ayyub Usta and Amin Usta. Image credit: Sunil Rampuria

Heritage Properties • 227

INSPIRATION

Enriching a Living Civilization

INSPIRATION

Enriching a Living Civilization

• Jaya Jaitly and Aman Nath

"As rhythm, whirl and melody merged seamlessly, the dervishes languished and lowered their arms from their chests. One arm lifted and its open palm faced skywards. The other arm was lowered and its palm faced towards the earth. The head lifted slightly... 'Life was all about balance,' a Sufi explained. The open palm of the whirling dervish that faced heavenwards received and the open palm facing downwards gave."

— Moin Mir, *The Lost Fragrance of Infinity*

And so is the balance of design, when it is open and inspirational. It is a many-faceted and many-splendoured fountainhead. The more one drinks, the more inspiration arrives. In the current context, craftspeople and designers bring their own elixirs: if one brings skill and dexterity, the other scale and drama, and the interactions can range from the subtle and sublime to those that bring utter bewilderment. But today, more than ever before, design is also about destabilizing that "balance."

Cultural intuitiveness first leads to the imagining of the forms. To this, the availability of natural materials in the proximity of the craftsperson adds both its strengths and weaknesses. After all, igloos are not made with sand grains. Then comes dexterity, coded into the DNA of generations of skill. But all these would mean nothing if inspiration was lacking: nowadays, sand filled in synthetic cement bags, reinforced with bars of torr steel, when used in concentric circles as if they were blocks of ice, can produce cool, sand igloos.

Once, limited exposure gave crafts their rootedness. Today, more exposure offers many possibilities for great new breakthroughs. But there are warnings about over-exposure, used without a designer's restraint, which risk a hybrid of over-aggression and exuberance.

So how can designers, both Indian and international, walk this tightrope and succeed? There can be no strict formulae for something so intangible and refined as good inspiration, nor something so arrogant as "good taste." One must stay clear of any such arrogance, especially if one comes from the "developed" world or the metropolis.

The "demonstrative" tendency of skilled fingers in India more often runs away with the flute than plays good music. Great products are often spoilt by over-working on them. The reason for this is perhaps a lack of confidence and a consequent tendency to over-compensate owing to a desire to be accepted. But developed, contemporary, urban sensibilities can often guide and save the craft before it is "completed." The raw and real is natural today! It is the unfinished product that dazzles more than the varnished, finished one. Such natural consumer products are not called half-baked any more and often fetch higher prices, such as the brown Kerala rice with its husk, raw Bhagalpur *tussar* silks and others. This is why tweeds worn the wrong side out are more stylish, and uncut

PREVIOUS PAGES
Inspirational quotes on metal plates provide a backdrop for lighting panels at a gym.
Image credit: The Grid Architects

stones set in Antwerp are more expensive compared to the rows of painfully faceted emeralds from the Jaipur lapidary studios. The lesson is that the blasé design world's sensibilities now desire less in more, not more and more of more.

But the nouveau riche have always directed taste with the whip of their wallets. And with this comes excess. With time, these fads too become collectable curiosity items as craftspeople see one generation through their subsistence/existence. Aspirational designs with heavy price tags serve their own purpose, but the essential mustn't get derailed. That "return" to the core values inherent to the skill and material of the craft is also a designer's challenge.

India's power of assimilation has ensured that it would "transform the sword-in-hand invader to the wine cup–bearing lover," as Moin Mir writes. The best tip for anyone seeking Indian inspiration is to watch craftspeople at work, in admiration and awe, keeping every creative pore open, inhaling the genius slowly and with humility. From that learning will arise more inspirational works.

One of the most exciting facets of the human mind is its ability to innovate, ideate, create and explore the unknown. In the world of crafts, as in astrophysics, the universe is vast. Every stream of cultural history and every individual skill offers new possibilities to imagine and discover newer possibilities still of applying a craft form. Many designers and professionals, in areas that compete in offering new ideas and experiences, are today delving into the talents of our traditional craftspeople, challenging them and re-awakening them to the new world of technologies and experimentation.

Practitioners of craft skills in today's times cannot afford to be large in scale on their own. Designers who work with them tend to begin tentatively and on a small scale. Very often, a small idea needs a larger environment and new kinds of opportunities to expand their canvas with confidence. The heartening aspect of this situation is that many architects and interior designers are searching among craftspeople to help them create that extra zing—that extra level of surprise and unexpected innovation that only crafts can bring to a custom-made, unique habitat.

The common saying that necessity is the mother of invention becomes a concept that can create many new inventions only if people believe it is necessary to keep age-old craft skills alive to honour India's cultural heritage, sustain valuable skills and livelihoods, and make uniqueness the norm rather than leaning towards the easier option of mechanized replications of the industrial world. The human soul cannot feel a sense of pleasure without some form of aesthetic stimulation around itself. This section on inspirational explorations and the sharing of ideas that suggest collaborations between craftspeople and professional designers is an effort to open many windows, if not doors, to possibilities that lie ahead.

Inspiration comes when one faces challenges. The comfortable world of the architect or designer comes from an understanding of structure, grids, templates and calculations. For the craftsperson, length may be the count of five fingers, an elbow's length or the distance from the tip of the nose to the tip of a finger. A measurement of quantity is from *andaaz*, a beautiful word meaning intuitive or inherent knowledge. Outcomes for a professional designer are predicted and standardized. For the craftsperson, it is always slightly different each time. When both engage with each other, the professional is challenged to adjust to imbalance, while the craftsperson must anticipate the need for finding balance. This mating dance in the face of challenge is what brings out inspiration. •

Inspiration

Rooshad Shroff, Material: Makrana marble, metal, wood

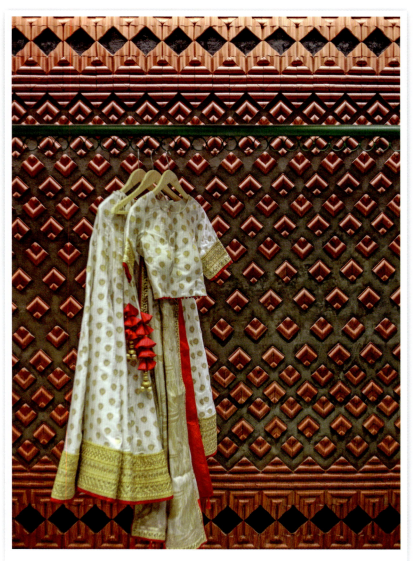

Manoj Patel Design Studio, Material: Clay, terracotta

Working towards contemporizing craft in order to make it relevant in today's design language, these marble bulbs and lamps are the result of a collaboration with artisans from Jaipur. Blocks of white Makrana marble are hollowed out into individual bulbs or tubes on the lathe. The surface of each bulb or lamp is further carved by hand with patterns inspired by crystal glass. The light passes through this carved texture in varying degrees, creating a unique effect. Such projects can introduce a renewed respect for traditional techniques, while conserving and extending craft know-how and honing it into a modern aesthetic.

Material: Makrana marble, metal, wood
Technique: Marble carving
Source Region: Rajasthan and Maharashtra, India
Studio: Rooshad Shroff

■ ■ ■

Clay roofing tiles were reinterpreted in a new design idiom and transformed into a wall mural to reflect the aesthetics of the space, a boutique store, by taking inspiration from the *pallu* of a sari, as well as ornamental *toran*s. Clay roofing tiles discarded at an earlier site were cut by hand into desired shapes and patterns. The material was bonded together chemically and then assembled into a wall mural. Given its flexibility, local artisans were able to shape it into myriad patterns, allowing for a great deal of customization. While clay itself is highly eco-friendly and low maintenance, the reuse of waste material enhanced the environmental responsiveness of this design.

Material: Clay, terracotta
Technique: Clay moulding, firing
Craftsperson(s): Tarachand Prajapati
Source Region: Gujarat, India
Studio: Manoj Patel Design Studio

■ ■ ■

Studio Tessera/rockpaperscissors, Material: Wood

"Rockpaperscissors" is an initiative to collect and reuse the large amounts of plywood waste generated by the construction and design industries, preventing this waste from ending up in a landfill. Through wood-turning on a lathe, the waste plywood is given form, after which, through traditional methods of woodworking, different finished products are created. The processes involved promote a deeper understanding of plywood and its properties, especially its cross-section, enabling a greater variety of experimental designs and skill updation for the designers and craftspeople involved, apart from the advantages of environmental sustainability.

Material: Wood
Technique: Wood-turning on lathe
Craftsperson(s): Irfan Mistry, Iqbal Mistry (wood craftsmen), Nasruddin Alam (wood-turning)
Source Region: Maharashtra, India
Studio: Studio Tessera/ rockpaperscissors

■ ■ ■

This project features the use of reclaimed wood scraps in the creation of exquisite flooring tiles for an art gallery. Wood was sourced from the joinery of old houses undergoing redevelopment in Ahmedabad. The reclaimed wood scraps were sorted by hand, de-nailed, planed and formed with tongue-and-groove joints as per the design. Each tile was handcrafted at the workshop and laid out, interlocked and fitted with headless nails on a plywood substrate at the site. The final flooring was planed, cleaned and sealed with Monocoat. In addition to using almost ten times less energy than virgin wood flooring, this process fixes the tiles without adhesives, enabling future reuse.

Material: Wood
Technique: Wood tilework
Craftsperson(s): Arjun Singhji, Soga Singhji
Source Region: Gujarat, India
Studio: Studio ārā

■ ■ ■

Studio ārā, Material: Wood

Inspiration • 233

Inspiration

Rice paper is made from the pith of the rice plant and not the actual rice grain that is eaten. This ensures that an otherwise inedible part of the plant is also used gainfully. The paper is pressed into sheets of thin, almost translucent paper and then printed with a colour-fast printing process. The artist Santanu Dey made this piece, which is a representation of the elements of the client's logo, keeping in mind the mathematical concept of the golden ratio. The processes employed were sustainable and eco-friendly. Rice paper of good quality enjoys longevity and its translucency and absorbency are also very consistent, making it long-lasting and durable.

Material: Burnt wood, canvas rice paper, acrylic on wood
Technique: Kaavad
Craftsperson(s): Santanu Dey
Source Region: New Delhi, India
Studio: Somaya and Kalappa Consultants

Somaya and Kalappa Consultants, Material: Burnt wood, canvas rice paper, acrylic on wood

■ ■ ■

A traditional practice of Mysore, Karnataka, marquetry is a technique of joining together pieces of wood to create visual stories. A composition is first designed and then drawn life-size by hand. The visual panels are original artworks created by ChippiWara Studio, or inspired by traditional Indian motifs. Expert artisans then identify the timber colours and grain patterns that are cut and placed to create a unique piece of marquetry. The cutting is done using a thin-blade saw, mostly by women. The panel is then glued and set under pressure till it becomes a single unified form. Cleaning, sanding and polishing are done to enhance the colours and grain patterns. The process uses reclaimed timber, which has a low carbon footprint and offers biophilic benefits, as well as pieces discarded from industrial use, ultimately providing the larger advantage of upcycling.

ChippiWara, Material: Wood

Material: Wood
Technique: Marquetry and inlay
Source Region: Karnataka, India
Studio: ChippiWara Studio

■ ■ ■

Studio Hinge, Material: Wood, resin

The design of this partition wall was conceptualized as a blend of many different craft forms, all invoking the client's roots in Rajasthan, with its beautiful *jaali*s and sand dunes. Birch ply was cut, and stylized holes or spaces for resin artwork were fitted in. The resin blocks were poured by hand by artists to cast plants, flowers and family memorabilia (like photographs), to create the impression of fossilized objects. All the objects thus cast were personal items belonging to the family, which brought warmth and a sense of belonging to the wall space. The resin was also custom-coloured using natural dyes. The entire design was assembled on site by craftsmen, carpenters and artists. Using birch ply made of FSC timber and natural dyes for the resin ensured a very low environmental impact for this project.

Material: Wood, resin
Technique: Wood carving, resin casting
Source Region: Maharashtra, India
Studio: Studio Hinge

■ ■ ■

Resist dyeing on textiles offers a great visual vocabulary. For this project, the wall surface featured a backdrop of textiles that were dyed using a variety of techniques, such as spotted *bandhej* or *shibori*. This was then combined with shaded dyeing and bleaching to achieve a textured, linear quality. Together, these techniques created a wonderful range of expressions and narratives. The fabrics used are naturally sustainable with

Inspiration

Spider Design, Material: Cotton, silk, khadi, satin, velvet, linen, coarse fabrics

azo-free dyeing techniques. Being textile-based, these designs can be easily maintained and upcycled or reused in time.

Material: Cotton, silk, khadi, satin, velvet, linen, and coarse fabrics
Technique: Resist dyeing
Source Region: Gujarat, Rajasthan and New Delhi, India
Studio: Spider Design

■ ■ ■

The Abhir Chair is a product born from the union of masculine teak and feminine textile. Made from original teak wood and the most organic form of cotton carpet, the Abhir is handcrafted with nature and design sensibilities, resulting in a chair with comfort, beauty and utility. The mastery of woodwork with natural teak wood is combined with the *kaarigari* of the *dari* weavers of Kutch in bespoke cotton textiles that integrates into the design. Reclaimed teak wood, with an eco-friendly finish, is used along with organic cotton on a handloom, making the Abhir Chair a sustainable product.

Material: Wood, cotton
Technique: *Dari* weaving, woodwork
Craftsperson(s): Virjibhai Vankar
Source Region: Gujarat, India
Studio: Tectona Grandis Furniture

■ ■ ■

Tectona Grandis Furniture, Material: Wood, cotton

DU Studio, Material: Textiles

"Textile Art by Kalai & Varsha" is a series that explores the work of contemporary women artists who work with artisans in traditional embroidery as well as new avenues of prints and cyanotype. Both these contemporary artists have created a niche for themselves and work from Delhi, Ahmedabad, Hyderabadand Sivakasi/Puducherry. These featured works were specially made for this boutique retail space as it connects very well with the idea of the tactile quality of textiles, in particular one that celebrates women and the sari. Most of the materials were locally sourced from regions in Gujarat and Puducherry, where the client is located. Given the low environmental impact of using traditional crafts and methods, the potential for reuse is very high.

Material: Textiles
Technique: *Tanka* embroidery, cyanotype
Craftsperson(s): Artisans working with Varsha Bagaria
Source Region: Gujarat, Tamil Nadu and Puducherry, India
Studio: Dustudio

■ ■ ■

Mural painting is a form of traditional storytelling that has been a presence in Kerala's rich architectural history for a long time. The mural we have showcased in our project narrates the story of Nalan and Damayanthi, as depicted in the Mahabharata, and has been done on the wall adjacent to the *puja* room. First, a mixture of lime and clean sand, and then a mixture of lime, sand and cotton, was used to plaster the wall with a beautiful white texture. Then the wall was washed with 25 to 30 coats of a mix consisting of quick lime and the juice of tender coconuts. After this, the outlines were made, colours were applied and then decorative detailing was done. All the materials embodied in this design, right from the preparation of the wall to the paint, were naturally sourced; being intrinsic to the environment, they were not only harmless but also a part of the natural ecosystem.

Material: Plant- and mineral-based pigments, lime, sand, cotton
Technique: Mural painting
Craftsperson(s): Sajan
Source Region: Kerala, India
Studio: BCA Architecture

■ ■ ■

Inspiration

BCA Architecture, Material: Plant- and mineral-based pigments, lime, sand, cotton

This gym features prominently a set of metal gears, which can be set in motion by pulling a set of chains, itself an exercise. This kinetic sculpture was meant to recall the action of drawing water from a well and was a subtle nod to the ceaseless activity in a fitness centre. Reclaimed MS plates with cutouts of inspirational mantras were used for lighting panels, which created interesting shadow play on the ceiling. The cladding was made of chains as a way of encouraging people to experience the tactility of the space. The added benefit of metal was that gradual oxidation would enhance the texture of the designs naturally. The use of reclaimed metal, LED lighting and recycled wood and rubber made this project very eco-friendly.

The Grid Architects, Material: Reclaimed MS, wood, rubber flooring, timber, glass

Moreover, the bio-philic design emphasized the need for oxygen-creating plants, further providing a connection to nature.

Material: Reclaimed MS, wood, rubber flooring, timber, glass
Technique: Metalwork
Source Region: Gujarat, India
Studio: The Grid Architects

The bejewelling technique of *meenakari*, traditionally done over silver or gold, has been applied here over sheets of copper. This ancient craft of copper enamelling, using glass-infused colours and intricate wire-motif workmanship, is unique to India. Copper sheets are cut to shape and then modelled into 3D objects, after which brilliantly coloured glass powders are fused on them. Whether it is to simulate delicate flowers on a garland, or koi fish in a lotus pond, these techniques help bring a sense of suspended animation to the pieces; for example, by adding flux to copper plates to hold the wire motifs in place. The wet-packing method is used to incorporate colours, and to do the final firing and cleaning. Copper is anti-microbial, recyclable and durable, and its use has supported the artisans and given them a sense of community.

Material: Copper
Technique: *Meenakari* and other forms of embellishing
Source Region: Maharashtra, India
Studio: Baaya Design

■ ■ ■

Baaya Design, Material: Copper

Inspiration • 239

Inspiration

Baaya Design, Material: Metal

Studio Moya
Material: Parchment leather

Depicting the ten unique incarnations of Lord Vishnu, this brass design of the *dashavatar* used the traditional *dhokra* lost-wax casting technique. The process involved intricate patterns that were generated with wax threads (with custom-made convex) and then replaced with hot molten brass, poured into moulds. The recycled brass was locally sourced. Wax for the moulds was prepared using a reusable mixture of paraffin, beeswax, tar and camphor. The clay used was sourced from Chhattisgarh and mixed with rice husk. Hence, the project used organic, biodegradable materials keeping in mind the benefits of the same as opposed to large-scale industrial procurements. The designs were conceptualized and executed under the guidance of the architect Shimul Kadri and Team Baaya.

Material: Metal
Technique: *Dhokra*, or lost-wax casting
Source Region: Chhattisgarh, India
Studio: Baaya Design

■ ■ ■

Tholu bommalata, a form of traditional leather puppetry, is a heritage craft from Andhra Pradesh and Telangana, narrating mythological tales with majestic, handcrafted leather puppets that dance against a backlit screen to a folk chorus. These lamps and light fixtures have been created using the traditional craft of leather puppetry in a contemporary mode. The parchment leather, which is the canvas of this craft, is sized and carefully stitched onto the metal frame. The drawings are then marked on it with a bamboo pen and coloured with drawing inks, all by hand. The artisans who worked on these products, D. Chinnarammana and his son Venkatesh, have a long multi-generational involvement in this craft. The tiny holes made after finishing the product add grandeur to the light once lit. The translucent nature of parchment leather makes it a very interesting material to explore the play of light around it. The leather used is sourced as waste from the food industry and given a new form.

Material: Parchment leather
Technique: *Tholu bommalata*, or leather puppetry
Craftsperson(s): D. Chinnarammana and Venkatesh
Source Region: Andhra Pradesh, India
Studio: Studio Moya

■ ■ ■

Viaanca Interiors, Material: Ethically sourced camel bones

S+PS Architects, Material: Paper

Handcrafted (ethically sourced) bone-inlay panels for a private residence feature a traditional floral pattern set in a green resin. One of the panels acts as a hidden door to a powder room in the entry foyer, with another panel added for symmetry. The process begins by cutting and delicately shaping bone fragments. These fragments are then set into a timber frame in a detailed pattern, after which a malleable material such as resin is filled around the pieces of bone/shell to create a contrasting background. The final process involves sanding and waxing to create a smooth finish. Ethically sourced bone-inlay furniture is sustainable since it involves the use of bones of camels that have passed away due to natural causes.

Material: Ethically sourced camel bones
Technique: Mosaic/bone inlay
Craftsperson(s): Narender/Variety Arts Emporium
Source Region: Rajasthan, India
Studio: Viaanca Interiors

■ ■ ■

Sanjhi is a form of traditional stencilled paper cutting, using a special small scissor, which produces exquisite designs and intricate motifs. The sliding glass door, seen here, was adjacent to the client's *puja* room. The *sanjhi*-patterned paper cutwork panel was sandwiched between the sliding glass doors to act as a screen. Since the partition screen was adjacent to the client's *puja* room, *sanjhi*, which comes from Mathura, the birthplace of Lord Krishna, seemed like an apt choice of craft to decorate the space. The artisans were also primarily based out of Mathura, which helped us underline the deep devotional ethos of the craft and its significance for the space.

Material: Paper
Technique: *Sanjhi* paper cutting
Craftsperson(s): Mohanji Mathurawale
Source Region: Uttar Pradesh, India
Studio: S+PS Architects

■ ■ ■

Inspiration • 241

Appendices

1. Crafts Directory

2. Interior Design Trade Associations

3. Educational Institutes offering Programmes in Interior Design

4. Crafts Associations and Organizations

5. Principal Committee and Contributors to the Book

Key to the Awards Bestowed on Craftspersons

(NA) National Award, awarded by the Government of India

(SA) State Award, awarded by State Governments

(MC) Merit Certificate, awarded by the Government of India

(SG) Shilp Guru, awarded by the Government of India

(NHA) National Handicraft Award, awarded by the Government of India

(SHA) State Handicraft Award

(PV) Padma Vibhushan, awarded by the Government of India

(PB) Padma Bhushan, awarded by the Government of India

(PS) Padma Shri, awarded by the Government of India

(VA) Vishwakarma Award

(LKNA) Lalit Kala National Award

Legends

- Stone
- Glazed Ceramics and Terracotta
- Grass, Coir and Natural Fibres
- Bamboo, Cane and Willow
- Wood
- Textiles
- Surface Decoration
- Metal
- Glass and Mirror-work

PB Punjab
HR Haryana
HP Himachal Pradesh
UK Uttarakhand
DL Delhi
RJ Rajasthan
UP Uttar Pradesh
BR Bihar
SM Sikkim
ML Meghalaya
AS Assam
AR Arunachal Pradesh
GJ Gujarat
MP Madhya Pradesh
CT Chhattisgarh
JH Jharkhand
OD Odisha
WB West Bengal
TR Tripura
MZ Mizoram
MN Manipur
NL Nagaland
GA Goa
KA Karnataka
TG Telangana
AP Andhra Pradesh
KL Kerala
TN Tamil Nadu

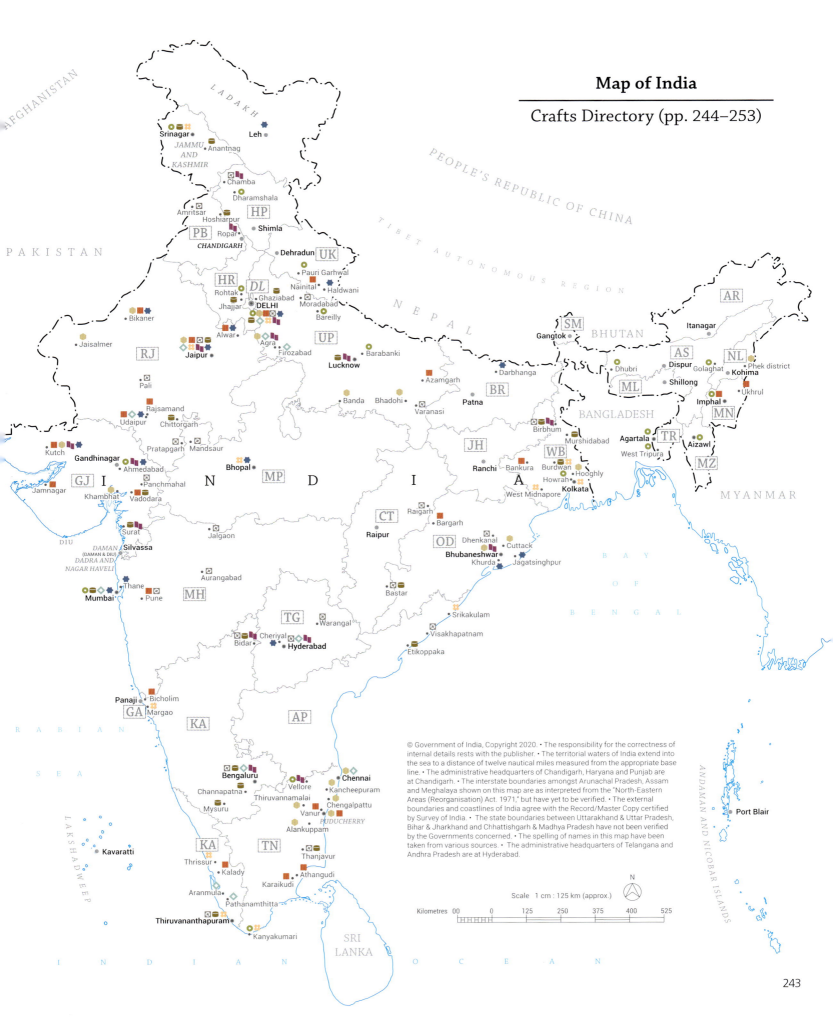

Crafts Directory

Stone

Stone carving
Delhi

- Latika Katt (LKNA) • Recognized by Gujarat State Lalit Kala Academy
  New Delhi, DL

Khambat beads
Gujarat

- Anwar Hussain Inayat Shaikh (NA)
  Khambat, GJ
  T: +91 9909290029 • +91 99787 67866

Stone carving
Odisha

- Sudarshan Sahoo (PV) • (PS) • (NA) • (SG)
  Bhubaneswar, OD
  T: +91 91 674 2360052 / 2360588
  E: sacvbbsr@gmail.com
  www.sudarshancrafts.com/#pioneer
- Kalpataru Maharana (SG) • (NHA)
  Cuttack, OD | T: +91 9438153090
- Keshava Maharana (SG)
  Bhubaneswar, OD | T: +91 986007025
- Raghunath Mohapatra (PB) • (PS) • (SG)
  Bhubaneshwar, OD

Stone carving and etching
Puducherry

- Gopi, Monolith Granites
  Alankuppam, PY | T: + 91 9489967322

Gemstone carving
Rajasthan

- Prithvi Raj Kumavat (NA) • (SA)
  Jaipur, RJ | T: +91 9828321516
  E: prithvikumawat@gmail.com

Stone carving
Rajasthan

- Raghav
  T: +91 9829063112

Stone naquashi
Rajasthan

- Tarun Veshnav
  Jaisalmer, RJ | T: +91 9799735580

Usta work/Manoti art
Rajasthan

- Ajmal Hussain Ustad
  Bikaner, RJ
  T: +91 94134 67471 • +91 97825 31367

Stone carving
Tamil Nadu

- V. Ganapathi Sthapathi (NA) • (SG)
  Chennai, TN | T: +91 44 4492651
- M. Devaraj Silpi (NA) • (SA)
  Kancheepuram, TN | T: +91 9444789814
  E: rajakkk2004@yahoo.com
- T. Bhaskaran
  Kancheepuram, TN
  T: +91 44 27442595 • +91 9443342097
  E: creativesculptors@yahoo.com
  www.creativesculptors.in
- S. Perumal Stapathi (NA) • (SG)
  Chengalpattu, TN | T: +91 44 4492651 •
  +91 9840395339 • +91 9043143887
- N. Mani Asari (SA)
  Thiruvannamalai, TN

Stone carving and jaali work
Uttar Pradesh

- Jay Kumar
  Bhadohi, UP | T: +91 9935347262

Marble inlay
Uttar Pradesh

- Hafiz Ahmed Khan (NA) • (SG)
  Agra, UP
- Iqbal Ahmed (NA) • (SG) • "The Greatest Artist,"
  the Australian Government (1980)
  Agra, UP | T: +91 9412256786
- Rafiquddin (NA) • (SG)
  Agra, UP | T: +91 9837131148

Shazar stone
Uttar Pradesh

- Dwarika Prasad Soni (NA) • (SA)
  Banda, UP

Stone dust work
West Bengal

- Sukhdeb Biswas (NHA)
  Hooghly, WB | T: +91 9836079433

Glazed Ceramics and Terracotta

Traditional pottery
Delhi

- Harkishan Prajapati (SG)
  New Delhi, DL | T: +91 9810397249

Red clay pottery
Goa

- Kamaldev S. Pandit
  Bicholim, GA | T: +91 0832 2362169
  E: goapotteries@gmail.com

Azulejos tiles
Goa

- Shankar Turi
  Bicholim, GA | T: +91 919822155409
  E: azul.turi@gmail.com

Clay moulding
Gujarat

- Tarachand Prajapati
  Vadodara, GJ | T: + 91 7383142515

Lime plaster
Gujarat

- Bhagwanji
  T: +91 9414170345

Pottery with black-and-white stippling
Gujarat

- Abdul Ibrahim (NA)
  Kutch, GJ
- Ramzubhai Kumbhar

Lippan kaam
Gujarat

- Gani Mara
  Kutch, GJ

Terracotta slabs
Gujarat

- Bhupatbhai, Dhrafa Studio
  Jamnagar, GJ | T: +91 9979399682

Clay and mud plastering, araish and lime plastering
Kerala

- Iyakat Ibrahim Muval
- Dawood Ibrahim Muval

Brickwork with perforations and metal casting
Kerala

- Vinu Daniel
  E: jobs.wallmakers@gmail.com •
  vinudaniel@gmail.com

Clay firing and oxidation
Kerala

- Rajani Pillai
  Kalady, KL | T: +919818346969
  E: kumbhamcollective@gmail.com
- Shalini
  T: +91 8281489089

Clay murals and sculptures
Kerala

- Lakshmi
  T: +91 9544232252
- Sundaran (clay mural work)
  T: +91 9947209074

Terracotta artwork
Maharashtra

- Clay Chronicles
  Pune, MH
  E: claychroniclesindia@gmail.com

Terracotta artwork
Manipur

- Phanjoubam Khema (MC)
  Imphal East, MN | T: +91 9863364875

Longpi black pottery (Ham)
Manipur

- Mathew Sasa
  Ukhrul, MN | T: +91 9818060802
- Machihan Sasa (SA) • (SG) • (NA) • (MC)
  Ukhrul, MN | T: +91 8413050701

Terracotta roof-tile animals
Odisha

- Manbodh Rana
  Bargarh, OD | T: +91 7381284727

High-fired ceramics
Puducherry

- Karan Kumar, Tharam Ceramics
  Auroville, PY | T: +91 9489967322

Rajasthani clay pottery
Rajasthan

- Om Prakash Galav Master Artisan of the
  Year, 2017, World Crafts Council • UNESCO
  Award of Excellence for Handicrafts (twice
  winner) • Beijing Craft Biennale Award, 2014,
  Chinese Artists' Association • (NA)
  Alwar, RJ | T: +91 9828220685
  E: omprakashgalav@gmail.com

Jaipur blue pottery
Rajasthan

- Gopal Saini (NA)
  Jaipur, RJ | T: +91 9887455826
  E: ramgopalbluepottery@gmail.com
- Kirpal Singh Shekhawat (SG) • (PS) • (NA)
  Jaipur, RJ | T: +91 141201127
- Madan Lal (SA)
  East Delhi, DL | T: +91 11 224475667 •
  +91 9582564527 • +91 7835260256

Molela wall murals
Rajasthan

- Laxmi Lal Kumha (MC)
  Rajsamand, RJ | T: +91 9828666952
- Jamnalal Prajapati
  T: +91 9829041935
  E: jamnaterracotta@gmail.com
- Dinesh Kumhar
  Rajsamand, RJ | T: +919352735002
  E: dineshmolela@yahoo.co.in
- Khem Raj Kumbhar (NA)
  Udaipur, RJ | T: +91 295385119

Clay firing and oxidation
Rajasthan

- Mohammad Hanif Ustad (NA) • (SA)
  Bikaner, RJ | T: +91 151 524214

Athangudi tiles
Tamil Nadu

- Mr Alex, Mr Arun
  T: +91 4565 281461 • +91 9842470603
  (Whatsapp)
  E: athanguditiles@gmail.com •
  athangudi_tiles@yahoo.com
- G. Subramaniam
  Karaikudi, TN | T: +91 4565 233 331 / 281339 •
  +91 9442229331 / 9442228331
  E: athangudipalacetiles@gmail.com

Mud-house building
Uttarakhand

- Shagun Singh
  Nainital, UK | T: +91 095409 37144

Black pottery
Uttar Pradesh

- Ram Jata Prajapati (NA), 1987 • (MC) • (SA)
  Azamgarh, UP
  T: +91 54 62284474 / 284612 •
  +91 9936698891
- Sohit Kumar Prajapati (NA)
  T: +91 8176875260 • +91 9455003617
  www.facebook.com/sohitkumar.prajapati.3
- Rajendra Prasad Prajapati (NA) (MC)
  Azamgarh, UP | T: +91 54622844 / 284612
- Shiv Ratan
  T: +91 7275212148
  E: shivratanprajapati1980@gmail.com

Terracotta lamps
West Bengal

- Rajesh Roy
  T: +91 9811034676
  E: rajesh.monali@gmail.com

Clay pottery and sculpture
West Bengal

- Baul Das Kumbhakar
  Bankura, WB
  T: +91 9734754423 • +91 9732108543
  E: rch.terracotta.panchmura@gmail.com
- Brajanath Kumbhakar
  Bankura, WB | T: +91 9732035729
- Pashupati Kumbhakar
  Bankura, WB

Crafts Directory

High-fired ceramics
Puducherry

- Rakhi Kane
  Vanur, TN

Terracotta lighting

- Manav Gupta
  www.manavgupta.in/
  E: scapesandisms@gmail.com •
  manavgupta@manavgupta.in •
  manavguptainstallations@gmail.com

Grass, Coir and Natural Fibres

Jute craft
Andhra Pradesh (also Telangana)

- Aba Ramanamma
  Srikakulam, AP

Tholu bommalata (leather puppetry)
Andhra Pradesh (also Telangana)

- K. Sreenivasulu (NA)
  AP | T: +91 8897291616
- V. Chinna Kullayappa (MC)
  AP

Sikki grass craft
Bihar

- Dhirendra Kumar (NA)
  T: +91 8298550138 | E: rachna.sikki@gmail.com

Coconut-based craft
Goa

- Bromeu Perreria
  Margao, GA | T: +91 9422846907

Papier-mâché ceilings
Kashmir

- Gulam Hyder Mirza (SG)
  Srinagar, JK | T: +91 9797986381
- Riyaz Ahmad Khan (NA)
  Srinagar, JK | T: +91 9018471755
  E: khanbrothers09@yahoo.com
- Zahid Hussain Beig (NA)
  Srinagar, JK
- Fayaz Ahmad Jan (PS)
  Srinagar, JK

Coconut-based craft
Kerala

- A. Prathap (NA)
  S.P.S. Handicrafts,
  Thiruvananthapuram, KL
  T: +91 471 2326145 • +91 9811261287
  E: babumanakkal@mail.com

Natural fibre and coir work
Kerala

- Swami Asparsananda
  T: +91 9447489229

Pattamadai/kora grass mats
Kerala

- Shri Ayyapan (International Craft Award)
  Thrichur, KL | T: +91 9544152413

Jute craft
Madhya Pradesh

- Meena Tiwari
  Bhopal, MP | T: +91 9826421249

Papier-mâché ceilings
Rajasthan

- Suman Soni (MC)
  Jaipur, RJ | T: +91 9314905918

Screw pine craft
Tamil Nadu

- Thanga Jothi (SA)
  Kanyakumari, TN | T: +91 9487550923

Coconut-shell carving (lamps)
West Bengal

- Rathindra Nath Malik (NA)
  Kolkata, WB | T: +91 9231922848
- Tapas Pal (SG)
  Burdwan, WB | T: +91 9734931888

Jute craft
West Bengal

- Rabin Ranja Dey (NA)
  WB

Masland mat weaving
West Bengal

- Tapas Kumar Janab (NA)
  West Midnapore, WB
  T: +91 9635178909 • +91 9434942166

Bamboo, Cane and Willow

Cane furniture
Assam

- Pradip Kumar Dey
  Dhubri, AS | T: +91 9957517466
- Sadanonda Das (NA)
  Golaghat, AS

Chik making
Delhi

- Ramji Lal (MC)
  New Delhi, DL
- Madan Singh (MC)
  New Delhi, DL

Jute rope making
Gujarat

- Pappubhai
  Ahmedabad, GJ | T: +91 9925721088
- Bhupendrabhai
  Ahmedabad, GJ | T: +91 9925040796

Sarkanda craft
Haryana

- Ram Swaroop (SA)
  Rohtak, HR

Cane crafts
Himachal Pradesh

- Vijay Kumar Mehra
  Dharamshala, HP | T: +91 9816377249

Wicker work
Kashmir

- Ab Rashid Rathar
  Srinagar, JK

Traditional weaving and cane craft
Maharashtra

- Siraj Ansari
  Mumbai, MH | T: +91 96546 37194
- Zubair Ansari
  Mumbai, MH | T: +91 86551 83226

Bamboo crafts
Manipur

- L. Shitraljit Singh (MC)
  T: +91 9402736001

▨ Kauna phak (reed mats)
Manipur

- **Akhom Raso Singh**
  Imphal, MN | T: +91 94029 87076

▨ Cane furniture
Mizoram

- **Lalthanzama Sailo** (NA)
  Aizawl, MZ

▨ Tazia making
Rajasthan

- **Azimuddin**
  T: +91 9024515313 • +91 9828031250

▨ Cane and wood furniture crafts
Tamil Nadu

- **C. M. Arumugam**
  Modimugan Cane Furniture, Vellore, TN
- **C. Thangajothi**
  Kanyakumari, TN | T: +91 9486550922

▨ Bamboo crafts
Tripura

- **Krishna Das Paul** (NA)
  Agartala, TR | T: +91 9862201042
- **Anita Das** (NA)
  Agartala, TR | T: +91 9436553609

▨ Bamboo crafts
Tripura

- **Tapan Chandra Das** (NA) • (SA)
  West Tripura, TR

▨ Cane furniture
Uttar Pradesh

- **Anil Kumar Sharma** (SA)
  Bareilly, UP
- **Ram Rati Verma** (SA)
  Barabanki, UP

▨ Lantana furniture
Uttarakhand

- **Dhiraj Singh Grahan**
  Pauri Garwal, UK
- **Vrijendra Choudhary**
  Pauri Garwal, UK

▨ Cane furniture
West Bengal

- **Jhunu Dutta**
  Howrah, WB | T: +91 9432278083

Wood

▨ Etikoppaka toys
Andhra Pradesh

- **C. V. Raju** (2nd National Grass-roots Innovation Award, National Innovation Foundation, India • Recognized by Craft Council of India and INTACH, Visakhapatnam • UNESCO Seal of Excellence • Kamala Devi Award)
  Etikoppaka, AP | T: +91-9701057267

▨ Bastar wood carving
Chhattisgarh

- **Jhitru** (NA)
  Bastar, CT
- **Kalipada Mondal** (MC)
  SEEDS India
  New Delhi, DL | T: +91 11 26174272
- **Pandi Ram Mandavi and Pichadu Ram**
  Bastar, CT | T: +91 9406284841

▨ Tuma/Duma craft—Burnt bamboo and wood etching
Chhattisgrah

- **Jagat Ram Devangan** (SA) • (MC)
  Bastar, CT
  T: +91 9755139614 • +91 9617832681
  E: dewangan_tumagudi@yahoo.com
- **Mangatra Netam**
  Bastar, CT | T: +91 7786244240

▨ Wood carving
Delhi

- **Mohammad Ayyub Khan** (SG) • (SHA)
  New Delhi, DL
  T: +91 9811842454 • +91 9686724798
  • +91 9555545457
  E: m.tahir4@gmail.com
  • mdtahir_92@yahoo.co.in

▨ Wood and bone inlay
Delhi

- **Omkar Dhawan** (NA) • (SA) • (SG)
  New Delhi, DL
  T: +91 11 22228418 • +91 9873648385
  • +91 9213706833

- **Narender** (bone inlay)
  Delhi | T: +91 9811048969

▨ Calligraphy in wood
Delhi

- **Irshad Hussain Farooqi** (SG) • (NA)
  New Delhi, DL
  T: +91 9968070070 • +91 9910577787
  E: calligraphycrafts@yahoo.com
  www.calligraphycrafts.com

▨ Lacquered wood-turning
Gujarat

- **Vadha Lalji Mal**
  Kutch, GJ | T: +91 9978014926

▨ Sankheda lacquerware
Gujarat

- **Himmatlal Mohan Lal**
  Lalit Sankheda Furniture, Vadodara, GJ

▨ Saadeli wood marquetry
Gujarat

- **Jitendra Petigara and Rakesh Petigara**
  Surat, GJ
  T: +91 9374542424 • +91 7016778982
  E: rakeshpetigara77@gmail.com

▨ Carpentry and upcycling
Gujarat

- **Paramjit Phull**
  T: +91 9228155515

▨ Wood carving
Haryana

- **Surya Kant** (MC)
  Jhajjar, HR | T: +91 9812189899

▨ Pinjrakari
Jammu & Kashmir

- **Mohammed Ashraf Bhat**
  Anantnag, JK

▨ Walnut wood carving
Jammu and Kashmir

- **Haji Abdul Aziz Bazaz**
  Srinagar, JK | T: +91 9797023498
- **Khalil Mohammad Kalwal** (SG) • (NA) • (MC)
  Srinagar, JK
  T: +91 97965 71717 • +91 9419005242

Crafts Directory • 247

Crafts Directory

🪵 Rosewood inlay
Karnataka

- **Jai Kumar** (Sri Lakshmi Handicrafts)
  Mysuru, KA
  T: +91 821-4260541 • +91 9845173669
  E: jaikumar9@hotmail.com
- **K. Mohan** (NHA)
  Mysuru, KA | T: +91 9886269174

🪵 Channapatna and wood-turned lacquerware
Karnataka

- **Suhel Parvez**
  Channapatna, KA
  T: +91 9108000881 • +91 99862 81007
  https://bharathartandcrafts.business.site/
- **K. Kenchaiah** (SA)
  Channapatna, KA | T: +91 9900509702
- **Syed Mubarak**
  T: +91 9845616078
- **Salimbhai**
  E: atuljohri@gmail.com

🪵 Wood marquetry or inlay
Karnataka

- **Faizur Rehman Khan** (NA) • (SA)
  Mysuru, KA | T: +91-821 2975519
  E: majeedfinearts@gmail.com
  www.majeedfinearts.com

🪵 Wood carving
Karnataka

- **Ashok Gudigar** (NA) • (SA) • (VA)
  Artisan Production Centre, Bengaluru, KA
- **M. Ramamurthy** (MC)
  Bengaluru, KA | T: +91-9845058344

🪵 Bidri work
Karnataka

- **Abdul Raouf** (SG) • (NA)
  Bidar, KA
  T: +91 90000 08317 • +91 99863 67541

🪵 Wood Carving
Kerala

- **R.V.Shajahan**
  Thiruvananthapuram, KL | T: +91 9748582643
- **K.R.Mohanan**
  Thiruvananthapuram, KL | T: +91 8606477930

🪵 Carpentry
Maharashtra

- **Bhagwan Suthar**
  Mumbai, MH | T: +91 9833993753

🪵 CNC cutting
Maharashtra

- **Pritesh Shah**
  T: +91 9987523990

🪵 Wood carving
Nagaland

- **Lhiwetsolo Kapfo** (MC)
  Phek district, NL | T: +91 9089337087

🪵 Wood carving
Punjab

- **Kamal Jit** (SHA)
  Hoshiarpur, PB | T: +91 7508033388
  E: matharukamal86@gmail.com

🪵 Wooden block making
Rajasthan

- **Gayour Ahmad** (SG)
  Jaipur, RJ | T: +91 9414821213

🪵 Tarkashi
Rajasthan

- **Mohan Lal Sharma** (NA) • (SA)
  Jaipur, RJ | T: +91 9460384023
- **Ram Dayal Sharma** (NA) • (SA) • (MC)
  Jaipur, RJ
  T: +91 141 2614899 • +91 9887147336
  E: avineshkumar.sharma17@gmail.com

🪵 Intricate sandalwood carving
Rajasthan

- **Kapil Jangid**
  Jaipur, RJ | T: +91 9214444550 •
  +91 9413995058 | E: jangidkapil1@gmail.com
  www.kapilhandicrafts.com/
- **Vinod Kumar Jangid** (SG)
  Jaipur, RJ | T: +91 9413995058

🪵 Kaavad
Rajasthan

- **Satya Narayan Suthar**
  Chittorgarh, RJ | T: +91 9829390239

- **Dwarkaji Prasad Jehangir** (Jangid)
  Chittorgarh, RJ
  T: +91 9829492503 • +91 3368706922
  E: dwarika.bassi@rediffmail.com

🪵 Rosewood carving
Rajasthan

- **Prithvi Raj Kumavat** (NA) • (SA)
  Jaipur, RJ | T: +91 9828321516
  E: prithvikumawat@gmail.com

🪵 Wire and wood inlay
Rajasthan

- **Mohan Lal Sharma** (NHA)
  Jaipur, RJ | T: +91 9460384023
- **Raghav, Dhoot Sangemermer**
  Jaipur, RJ | E: akd@dhootstonecraft.com

🪵 Sankheda lacquerware
Uttar Pradesh

- **Faraaz Aqeel** (NA) • (SA) • (Vishwakarma)
  Ghaziabad, UP
  T: +91 983737473240 • +91 9368478020
  E: info@sajavathandicraft.com •
  sajavathandicraft.com

🪵 Bone carving
Uttar Pradesh

- **Abdul Khaliq** (NA)
  Lucknow, UP
- **Jalaluddin** (NA) • (SA)
  Lucknow, UP
  T: +919415763120 • +91 9807333035

🪵 Wood carving
West Bengal

- **Dhruba Sil**
  Burdwan, WB | T: +91 9233126428

🪵 Sholapith work
West Bengal

- **Ananta Malakar** (NA) • (SA) • (SG) • (MC)
  Birbhum, WB | T: +91 9732025529 •
  +91 9474868641 • +91 9474868681
- **Samir Saha**
  Murshidabad, WB | T: +91 9832231113
- **Kamal Malakar**
  Birbhum, WB | T: +91 9474009311

Textiles

Kalamkari
Andhra Pradesh

- K. Siva Prasada Reddy (SG)
  AP

Kalamkari
Assam

- Ajit Kumar Das (NA) · (SA)
  AS

Block printing
Delhi

- Dhvani Behl (Flora for Fauna)
  New Delhi, DL

Khatli embroidery
Gujarat

- Ehsanali Shaikh
  Surat, GJ | T: +91 8866273193

- Gulambhai Jariwala
  Royal Embroidery
  Surat, GJ | T: +91 9427135288

Bandhani, or tie-and-dye dyeing
Gujarat

- Shakur Khatri (MC)
  GJ | T: +91 288 2672670 · +91 9898234819

- Mahmed Yakub Khatri (NA)
  Kutch, GJ | T: +91 9409473025

Patola weaving
Gujarat

- Pankajbhai D Makwana (NA)
  GJ | T: +91 2752 33378 · +91 9898252171

Ajrakh printing
Gujarat

- Dr. Ismail Khatri (NA)
  GJ | T: +91 9879334200
  E: irfankhatri2006@yahoo.co.in

Rogan painting
Gujarat

- Arab Hasam Khatri (NA)
  Kutch, GJ | T:+91 9879425812
  E: traditionalroganart@gmail.com

- Sumar D. Khatri (NA)
  Kutch, GJ

Batik
Gujarat

- Sudhir V. Phadnes (NA)
  Delhi, DL
  T: +91 9868104106 · +91 9999326673
  E: sudhirphadnes@gmail.com

- Shakil Ahmed Kasambhai Khatri (NA)
  GJ

- Jaba Champaneria, Kuryaat Arts
  Surat, GJ | T: +91 9998981217

Appliqué
Gujarat

- Tejiben Makwana (NA)
  GJ

- Mrugen Rathod (artist)
  Ahmedabad, GJ | T: +91 9825885158
  E: mrugen2340@gmail.com

- Rajesh Sharma
  Ahmedabad, GJ | T: +91 9979741618

Ari embroidery
Gujarat

- Vankar Lachhuben Becharlal (NA)
  Kutch, GJ

Kutch embroidery
Gujarat

- Geetaben Vikram Balasara (NA)
  Kutch, GJ

Durrie weaving
Gujarat

- Harjibhai Manjibhai (SA)
  Kutch, GJ

Chamba rumaal
Himachal Pradesh

- Lalita Vakil (NA) · (SG)
  HP | T: +91 1899 22707

Kashidakari embroidery
Jammu and Kashmir

- Mohammed Iqbal
  JK | T: +91 9868670924

Tibetan carpets and Navalgund rugs
Karnataka

- Abdul Hakeem (MC)
  Bidar, KA

Appliqué
Karnataka

- Mehr Seth
  Bengaluru, KA | E: mehr.seth@gmail.com

Banjara embroidery
Karnataka

- Praveen Nayak
  KA | T: +91 08395 260208/207

Kasuti embroidery
Karnataka

- Usha J. Pawar (NA)
  KA | T: +91 9845078141 · +91 8023366522
  E: ushapawar@hotmail.com

Block printing of Bagh
Madhya Pradesh

- Abdul Kadar Khatri (NA)
  MP

Artistic textiles
Manipur

- Anoubam Kalpana Devi (NA)
  MN | T:+91 9856108728

Pipili appliqué
Orissa

- Shantilata Parida (SA)
  Bhubaneshwar, OD

Knitting
Pan-India

- Neha Bhardwaj
  New Delhi, DL

Panja rugs
Punjab

- Kartar Kaur (SA)
  Ropar, PB

Phulkari and embroidery
Punjab

- Paramjeet Kaur Kapoor (NA)
  PB

Bandhej dyeing
Rajasthan

- Khatri Abdul Shakur Osman (NA)
  GJ | T: +91 2834 224307 · +91 9426967891

Crafts Directory • 249

Crafts Directory

Leheriya, or tie-resist dyeing
Rajasthan

- Haji Badshah Miyan (NA) · (SG)
  RJ | T: +91 141 2303845 ·+91 9414323984 ·
  +91 94143239843
  E: badshahmiyan@gmail.com

Dabu mud-resist printing
Rajasthan

- Lalchand Derawala (NA)
  Jaipur, RJ

Woollen druggets
Tamil Nadu

- B A Venkataraman
  Vellore, TN

Tanka embroidery
Telangana

- Varsha Bagaria
  Hyderabad, TG | T: +91 8897467890

Knotted carpets
Uttar Pradesh

- Akhtar Bano (NA)
  Agra, UP

Chikankari embroidery
Uttar Pradesh

- Shweta Kaistha (NA)
  New Delhi, DL | T: +91 9818182950

Zardozi, or golden thread embroidery
Uttar Pradesh

- Iqrar Husain Rizvi (NA)
  UP | T: +91 9335215364
  E: syediqrarhusainrizvi@gmail.com
- Mohd. Bilal (MC)
  UP | T: +91 9258731716

Kantha, or patched cloth embroidery
West Bengal

- Mahamaya Sikdar (NA)
  WB | T: +91 9874056381
- Tripti Mukharjee (SG)
  Birbhum, WB | T: +91 9434041026
  E: triptimukharjee.2007@rediffmal.com

Surface Decoration

Madhubani painting
Bihar

- Asha Jha (NA)
  Darbhanga, BR | T: +91 8987384973

Mithila lokchitra
Bihar

- Hema Devi (NA)
  BR | T: +91 9006362222 · +91 9934076609
  E: arthema123@gmail.com

Mithila lokchitra
Delhi

- Mamta Devi (NA)
  New Delhi, DL | T: +91 7065581455
  E: mamtadevi@gmail.com

Mata ni Pachhedi painting
Gujarat

- Bhanubhai Chunilal Chitara
  Ahmedabad, GJ | T: +91 9898110165

Lippan kaam
Gujarat

- Gani Mara
  Kutch, GJ

Thangka painting
Himachal Pradesh

- Tenzin Lama
  Ladakh | T: +91 8082325119 · +91 8219866317

Ganjifa art
Karnataka

- Vinutha Prakash (NA)
  KA | T: +91 9845438378

Kerala mural paintings
Kerala

- Sadaanandan P.K. (AT Abu Memorial Award)
  T: +91 9895203078 · +91 7034169165
  E: sadanandan.pk@gmail.com

Gond painting
Madhya Pradesh

- Ramesh Tekam (NA)
  MP | T: +91 9826016884
  E: rameshtekam1995@gmail.com
- Nankusia Bai (SA)
  MP

- Durgabai Vyam (NA)
  Bhopal, MP
- Kaushal Prasad Tekam
  Bhopal, MP | T: +91 918462841176
- Dilip Shyam
  Bhopal, MP

Pithora painting
Madhya Pradesh

- Bhuri Bai and Jor Singh
  Bhopal, MP | T: +91 755 2551878 / 2760668 ·
  +91 9893732027

Bhil art
Madhya Pradesh

- Geeta Bhariya
  MP | T: +91 9893390609 · +91 9179417614

Mandana art
Madhya Pradesh

- Kaluram Verma
  Bikaner, RJ
  T: +91 9828057164 · +91 8561877019
  E: marukalavant@gmail.com

Contemporary artwork
Maharashtra

- Ratna Gupta
  Mumbai | T: +91 9820091749

Warli painting
Maharashtra

- Jivya Soma Mashe (PS) · (SG)
  Thane, MH
  T: +91 9028631853 · +91 8975391497
  E: mhase2013@gmail.com

Patachitra painting
Odisha

- Dwijabar Das (MC)
  Khurda, OD | T: +91 9861062428
- Umesh Chandra Behra (MC)
  Jagatsinghpur, OD
- Saila Moharana (SG)
  T: +91 890849025

Bhittichitra wall painting
Rajasthan

- Radhe Shywam Rajwade
  RJ | T: +91 9165631546
- Santosh Kumar Yadav
  RJ | T: +91 9669347616

Miniature painting
Rajasthan

- **Shyamu Ram Dev** (MC)
  Jaipur, RJ | T: +91 9829047593
- **Reva Shankar Sharma**
  (National Master Craftsman Award)
  Udaipur, RJ | T: +91 9252206159
- **Babu Lal Marotia** (SG)
  Jaipur, RJ | T: +91 9829061804
  E: babulalmarotia@yahoo.com
- **Zenul Khan**
  Udaipur, RJ | T: +91 9462515149 •
  +91 7014775632

Phad painting
Rajasthan

- **Shamsher Khan** (NA) • (SA)
  Udaipur, RJ | T: +91 9982838015

Pichhwai, or painted temple hangings
Rajasthan

- **Rajaram Sharma** (NA)
  T: +91 9414161763
  E: rrchitrashala@yahoo.com

Cheriyal scroll painting
Telangana

- **D. Vaikuntam** (NA)
  TG | T: +91 9704519636 • +91 9949330262
  E: rakeshnakash@gmail.com
  www.vaikuntamnakash.blogspot.com/
- **D. Saikiran**
  Cheriyal, TG | T: +91 8125284264 •
  +91 8125284246

Sanjhi, or stencil paper cutting
Uttar Pradesh

- **Ram Soni**
  Alwar, RJ | T: +91 9829231175
  E: sanjhi.soni@gmail.com

Aipan, or ritual floor painting
Uttarakhand

- **Abhilasha Paliwal**
  Haldwani, UK | T: +91 7900688073
  E: parvatajan@gmail.com

Patachitra scroll painting
West Bengal

- **Anwar Chitrakar** (NA)
  T: +91 9733700769

- **Kalpana Chitrakar** (NA)
  WB | T: +91 9733647843 • +91 9732742028

Metal

Bronze casting
Andhra Pradesh

- **Makavarapallem Srinivas Rao**
  Visakhapatnam, AP

Dhokra lost-wax casting
Chhattisgarh

- **Sonadhar Poyam Vishwakarma**
  Bastar, CT
  T: +91 778642483 • +91 778642401
- **Bhupendra Baghel**
  Bastar, CT | T: +91 9425595341
  jbaghel@rediffmail.com
- **Rajendra Baghel** (NA)
  Bastar, CT | T: +91 9424291982
- **Govind Ram Jhara** (SG)
  Raigarh, CT | T: +91 9755795143

Iron craft
Chhattisgarh

- **Tiju Ram Vishwakarma** (NA) • (SA)
  Bastar, CT | T: +91 7786244089 •
  +91 9424291825 • +91 7089927867
  E: tijuramv@rediffmail.com

Brass craft
Delhi

- **Chanchal Chakraborty** (NHA)
  New Delhi, DL | T: +91 9560023695

Metal craft
Delhi

- **Jagdish Prasad** (SG) • (NHA)
  New Delhi, DL | T: +91 9990262448 •
  +91 11 23230543 • +91 9990262448

Chintaai silverware
Delhi

- **Mohammad Alam Warsi**
  Old Delhi, DL

Metal work
Gujarat

- **Yunus Luhar**
  GJ | T:+91 9601324323

- **Mahendrasinh Manubhai Gohil**
  Panchmahal, GJ | T:+91 9998011845

Mohra metal craft
Himachal Pradesh

- **Prakash Anand** (NA)
  Chamba, HP

Bidri work
Karnataka

- **Shah Rasheed Ahmed Quadri** (NA) • (SA) •
  Karnataka Rajyotsava Award • Great Indian
  Achievers Award • (SG)
  Bidar, KA | T: +91 9986796379
- **M. A. Raoof** (NA) • (SG)
  Bidar, KA

Bronze lost-wax casting
Karnataka

- **T.M. Mayachar** (NHA)
  Bengaluru, KA | T: +91 9341271895

Copper etching
Kashmir

- **Manzoor Ahmed Naquasheer**
  T: +91 9906499126

Vedic metal art
Kerala

- **Sivakumar S.R.** (NHA)
  Thiruvananthapuram, KL | T: +91 8089137960

Thewa craft
Madhya Pradesh

- **Ganpat Soni** (NA) • (SA)
  Mandsaur, MP
  T: +91 7421238398 • +91 9425979198
  E: thevaart_soni2005@yahoo.com

Tambat craft
Maharashtra

- **Balchandra Kadu**
  Pune, MH | T: +91 9168978684

Bidri work
Maharashtra

- **Madhukar Gawai**
  Aurangabad, MH | T: +91 9226217864
  • +91 9370774091 • +91 240-6547909
  E: madhubidri@yahoo.co.in

Crafts Directory

Bronze casting
Maharashtra

- Ramakant Roopchand Suryawanshi
  (SG) · (NHA) · (SHA)
  Jalgaon, MH | T: +91 9270722136

Dhokra lost-wax casting
Odisha

- Sansari Gadatia
  Dhenkanal, OD | T: +91 9938913656
- Son Singh Vishwakarma
  T: +91 9340138871 (also for Whatsapp) ·
  +91 9303191936 | E: kalabastar@gmail.com

Thathera craft
Punjab

- Mandeep Kumar Thathera
  Amritsar, PB

Meenakari
Rajasthan

- Jaswant Kumar Meenakar
  T: +91 9509076210 · +91 141 2569665
- Inder Singh Kudrat (SG) · (SHA) · (NHA)
  Jaipur, RJ
  T: +91 141 2620007 · +91 9928362291
  E: harminderdesign@gmail.com
- Kailash Soni (SG)
  Jaipur, RJ
  T: +91 141 4037225 · +91 9672998232
  E: kapilsia@gmail.com

Copper engraving, or marori work
Rajasthan

- Altaf Ali (NA)
  Jaipur, RJ

Koftgari
Rajasthan

- Rajesh Gahlot
  Pali, RJ | T: +91 7726065279

Thewa craft
Rajasthan

- Giresh Raj Soni (NA) · (SA) · (SG) · UNESCO Seal
  of Excellence)
  Pratapgarh, RJ
  T: +91 9425369227 · +91 74 22224545
  E: girish_thewaart@yahoo.com

Thanjavur plate art
Tamil Nadu

- Mari Muthu (senior craftsman)
  T: +91 9444803123

Swamimalai bronze icons
Tamil Nadu

- Devasenapathy Sthapathy
  Thanjavur, TN

Bidri work
Telangana

- Mohd Kareem Khan (NA) · (SA) · (MC)
  Hyderabad, TG
- Mohd Najeeb Khan (NA) · (SA) · (MC)
  Hyderabad, TG
  T: +91 40 214163 · +91 9811119453

Gold-leaf painting
Andhra Pradesh

- P.G. Keshavulu (NHA)
  Hyderabad, TG
  T: +91 9246533324 · +91 9440114333

Sheet metal artwork (brass)
Telangana

- R.Venkateshwarlu (NHA)
  Hyderabad, TG | T: +91 9246508048

Pembarti brassware
Telangana

- Ayla Achari
  Silver Industrial Coop Society Ltd.
  Warangal, TG

Copper repoussé craft
Uttar Pradesh

- Santosh | T: +91 9336915723
- Anil Kumar Kasera | T: +91 9450015863

Gulabi meenakari
Uttar Pradesh

- Ramesh Vishwakarma
  Jatan Shree Handicraft, Varanasi, UP
  T: +91 9839318227
- Kunj Bihari Singh (NA)
  Varanasi, UP

Brasswork and ashtadhatu work
Uttar Pradesh

- Anant Kumar Jain
  E: jainmetalsmbd@gmail.com

Metal engraving
Uttar Pradesh

- Man Mohan Soni (NHA)
  Mahooba, UP | T: +91 9450274674
- Harpal Singh Yadav (NHA)
  Moradabad, UP | T: +91 9410603467

Brass and bell-metal suri work
West Bengal

- Bholanath Karmakar (NHA)
  Birbhum, WB | T: +91 9732243326

Glass and Mirror-work

Glass art
Delhi

- Atul Bakshi
  New Delhi, DL
  T: +91 11 2613 9408 · +91 9811014904
  E: studioleadlight@gmail.com
  http://atulbakshi.com/

Glass blowing
Delhi

- Reshmi Dey
  New Delhi, DL | T: +91 9811992770
  E: contact@glasssutra.com ·
  glasssutrateam@gmail.com

Mirror-studded painting
Karnataka

- Vijaya Gopinath (MC) · Dasara Exhibition
  Awards for Mysore Paintings (four-time
  winner) and Dasara Exhibition Awards for
  Ganjifa, Karnataka Exhibition Authority ·
  Karnataka Lalit Kala Academy Award)
  T: +91 9972095345
  E: vijayagopinath9@gma l.com

Aranmula kannadi (mirrors)
Kerala

- T. N. Sivankutty (master craftsman)
Pathanamthitta, KL | T: +91 46 82313902 •
+91 9847144154 • +91 9447705036
• +91 9846696984
E: aravindaranmula@gmail.com
www.aranmulakannadionline.com

- Gopa Kumar
Pathanamthitta, KL
T: +91 46 82319031 • +91 9847461462
E: info@aditimetalmirror.com
E: gopanaranmulai@gmail.com
www.aditimetalmirror.com

- Sudhammal J.
Pathanamthitta, KL
T: +91 9605450518 • Whatsapp:
+91 9605468528
aranmulakannadi.co.in/
aranmulamirror.in/

- A. K. Selvaraj (master craftsman)
Aranmula, KL | T: +91 9947725232

Acrylic carving
Maharashtra

- Nalini Vijay Mehta (NA)
Mumbai, MH | T: +91 22 24094186
E: info@nalinimehtastudio.com
www.nalinimehtastudio.com

Stained-glass restorations, painting and etching
Maharashtra

- Swati Chandgadkar
Mumbai, MH

- Cyrus Jassawalla and Jaishree Karani
Mumbai, MH | T: +91 022 24138873
• +91 9820 135 462 • +91 9920 989 402
E: cyjay@cyjay-stainedglass.com

- Hema Desai
Mumbai, MH | T: +91 22 24168487/24163824
E: krutiglass@gmail.com
https://www.kruticreations.com

Thikri work
Rajasthan

- Rajesh Anant
Udaipur, RJ | T: +91 9414163368 •
+917742128547
E: anantrajesh@gmail.com

- Kishan
T: +91 9829702392

Mirror-studded painting
Rajasthan

- Badri Narain Marotia (NA) • (SA)
Jaipur, RJ | T: +91 9414229080
• +91 9414229080

- Shyam Sharma
Udaipur, RJ

Glass ceilings
Rajasthan

- Sabulal Panwar (NA) • (SA)
T: + 91 7568819576
E: panwarsabulal@gmail.com

Glass blowing
Tamil Nadu

- V. Srinivasa Raghavan
Chennai, TN
T: +91 44 22473210 • +91 9383473210
E: raagparadise@vsnl.net •
raagparadise@yahoo.co.in

Glass blowing
Telangana

- Syed Jaffer Ali Zaidi (SA)
Hyderabad, TG

Glass blowing
Uttar Pradesh

- Ghanshyam
Agra, Uttar Pradesh
T: +91 9411002694 • +91 8394808704

- Mahesh Kumar Kushwaha (SA)
Firozabad, UP
T: +91 9411002694 • +91 6395798764
E: mahesh2010chandra@yahoo.com

Interior Design Trade Associations

- **Association of Indian Design Industry**
  Bengaluru, KA
  www.web.archive.org/web/20080516182635/
  www.aidionline.org/
  Contact: sneha@aidionline.org

- **Architect and Interiors India**
  Mumbai, MH
  www.architectandinteriorsindia.com/projects
  Contact: indrajeet.saoji@itp.com

- **Association of Designers of India**
  Pune, MH
  www.adi.org.in/
  Contact: anshu.ajmani@
  associationofdesignersofindia.org

- **Crafts Council of India**
  Chennai, TN
  www.craftscouncilofindia.org
  Contact: +91 44 2434 1456

- **Delhi Crafts Council**
  New Delhi, DL
  www.delhicraftscouncil.org/
  Contact: delhicraft@gmail.com

- **Design India**
  Pune, MH
  www.design-india.com/
  Contact: info@design-india.com

- **Direct Create**
  New Delhi, DL
  www.directcreate.com/craft
  Contact: contact@directcreate.com

- **Institute of Indian Interior Designers**
  Mumbai, MH
  www.iiid.in/
  Contact: ho@iiid.in

- **Industree**
  Bengaluru, KA
  www.industree.org.in/
  Contact: info@industree.org.in

- **The Future of Design**
  Mumbai, MH
  www.tfod.in/
  Contact: support@tfod.in

- **The Guild of Designers and Artists**
  New Delhi, DL
  www.guild-designers-artists.com/
  Contact: theguildofdesigners@gmail.com

Educational Institutes offering Programmes in Interior Design

- **AAFT School of Interior Design**
  Noida, UP
  www.aaft.com/schoolofinterior/
  4 year course

- **Amity School of Design**
  Noida, UP
  www.amity.edu/asd/default.asp
  4 year course

- **Arvindbhai Patel Institute of Environmental Design (APIED)**
  Vidyanagar, GJ
  http://www.apied.edu.in/home.aspx
  4 year course

- **ARCH College of Design and Business**
  Jaipur, RJ
  www.archedu.org/
  4 year course

- **School of Design, CEPT University**
  Ahmedabad, GJ
  www.cept.ac.in/
  5 year course

- **Hindustan Institute of Technology and Science**, New Delhi, DL
  www.hindustanuniv.ac.in/
  4 year course

- **India Institute of Art and Design (IIAD)**
  New Delhi, DL
  www.iiad.edu.in/
  5 year course

- **ITM University Gwalior**
  Gwalior, MP
  www.itmuniversity.ac.in/
  3 year course

- **Jain University School of Interior Design**
  Bengaluru, KA
  www.jainuniversity.ac.in/
  3 year course

- **Lovely Professional University**
  Phagwara, PB
  www.lpu.in/
  4 year course

- **Manipal School of Architecture and Planning**
  Manipal, KA
  https://manipal.edu/mu.html
  4 year course

- **MVP Samaj's College of Architecture**
  Nashik, MH
  https://cansnashik.org/
  4 year course

- **P. P. Savani University**
  Surat, GJ
  https://ppsu.ac.in/sod/
  4 year course

- **Pearl Academy**
  New Delhi, DL
  https://pearlacademy.com/
  4 year course

- **Sharda University (School of Architecture and Planning) SAP**
  Noida, UP
  https://www.sharda.ac.in/schools/
  architecture-planning
  4 year course

- **Srishti Manipal Institute**
  Manipal, KA
  http://srishtimanipalinstitute.in/
  3 year course

- **Unitedworld Institute of Design (UID)**
  Gandhinagar, GJ
  https://karnavatiuniversity.edu.in/uid/
  4 year course

- **UPES School of Design**
  Misraspatti, UK
  https://www.upes.ac.in/
  4 year course

- **Vogue Institute of Art and Design**
  Bengaluru, KA
  https://www.voguefashioninstitute.com/
  3 year course

Crafts Associations and Organizations

- **All India Artisans' and Craftworkers' Welfare Association (AIACA)**
  New Delhi, DL
  T: +91 11 26272492/26270493/94
  E: contact@aiacaonline.org
  www.aiacaonline.org/

- **Arch Institute of Design and Business**
  Jaipur, RJ
  T: +91 9351337770
  www.archedu.org/b-des-craft-accessory-design.html

- **Bamboo Research and Training Centre,**
  Chandrapur, MH
  T: +91 9552729996 • +91 7172 272999
  E: directorbrtc@mahaforest.gov.in
  www.brtc.org.in/

- **Cauvery Crafts from Karnataka**
  Bengaluru, KA
  T: +91 80 25582793/71204445/71204446
  E: md@cauveryhandicrafts.net
  www.cauverycrafts.com/index.html

- **Craft Development Institute**
  Srinagar, JK
  T: +91 194 2411430/2411772
  E: cdi@cdisgr.org
  www.cdisgr.org/contact.html

- **Delhi School of Art**
  New Delhi, DL
  T: +91 11 41054287 • +91 8860264505
  • +91 9871188405
  E: info@delhischoolofart.com
  www.delhischoolofart.in/

- **Desh Bhagat University**
  Fatehgarh Sahib, PB
  T: +91 8283811111
  E: contact@deshbhagatuniversity.in
  www.deshbhagatuniversity.in/design/diploma-in-art-and-craft

- **Government College of Art and Craft**
  Kolkata, WB
  T: +91 33 22522479/22522186
  E: gcackolkata150@gmail.com
  www.gcac.edu.in

- **Handicrafts and Carpet Sector Skills Council,**
  New Delhi, DL
  T: +91 11 26133165/26139834
  E: ceo@hcssc.in | www.hcssc.in/

- **Himanshu Art Institute**
  New Delhi, DL
  T: +91 9810425823
  E: info@himanshuartinstitute.co.in
  www.himanshuartinstitute.co.in/

- **India Crafts**
  www.india-crafts.com/

- **Indian Institute of Carpet Technology**
  Srinagar, JK
  T: +91 194 2411143
  www.iictsrinagar.org/

- **Indian Institute of Crafts and Design**
  Jaipur, RJ
  T: +91 141 2701203/2701504/2700156
  E: info@iicd.ac.in | www.iicd.ac.in/en/

- **Indira Gandhi National Centre for the Arts,**
  New Delhi, DL
  T: +91 11 23388460
  E: igncapub@gmail.com
  www.ignca.gov.in/

- **Institute of Fine Arts, Chandigarh**
  Chandigarh, PB
  T: +91 9872822690
  www.instituteoffinearts.co.in/

- **Institute of Wood Science and Technology,**
  Bengaluru, KA
  T: +91 80 22190100/22190200
  E: dir_iwst@icfre.org • director.iwst@gmail.com
  www.iwst.icfre.gov.in/

- **Jnana-Pravaha Institute**
  Mumbai, MH

- **Jyoti Vidyapeeth Women's University**
  Jaipur, RJ
  T: +91 141 2370501
  E: admission@jvwu.ac.in •
  registrar@jvwu.ac.in • dsd@jvwu.ac.in
  www.jvwu.ac.in/directorate-of-skill-development.html

- **Maharani Kishori Jat Kanya Mahavidyalaya,**
  Rohtak, HR
  E: mkjkmrtk@gmail.com
  www.mkjkcollege.org/

- **Mahatma Gandhi Institute for Rural Industrialization**
  Wardha, MH
  T: +91 7152 253512/13 • +91 7152 253513
  E: director.mgiri@gmail.com
  www.mgiri.org/

- **National Bamboo Mission**
  New Delhi, DL
  T: +91 11 23389023
  E: singhranjit@cag.gov.in
  www.nbm.nic.in/Green-Ideas.aspx

- **National Institute of Design**
  Ahmedabad, GJ
  T: +91 79 2662 9500
  www.nid.edu/education/bachelor-design.html

- **National Institute of Fashion Technology,**
  New Delhi, DL
  T: +91 11 26542000 | www.nift.ac.in/

- **National Skills Network**
  Hyderabad, TG
  E contact@nationalskillsnetwork.com
  www.nationalskillsnetwork.in/craft-training-institutes-higher-education-and-skills/

- **Savitri Polytechnic for Women**
  Faridabad, HR
  T: +91 88005 91561 • +91 9810373703
  E: info@savitripolytechnic.co.in
  www.savitripolytechnic.co.in/

- **Skill India NSDC**
  New Delhi, DL
  T: +91 11 47451600–10
  E: support.smart@nsdcindia.org •
  skillindia.helpdesk@nsdcindia.org
  www.skillindia.nsdcindia.org/

- **South Delhi Polytechnic for Women**
  New Delhi, DL
  T: +91 11 26294833/26294836 •
  +91 11 41080048
  E: southdelhipolytech@gmail.com •
  director@southdelhipolytechnic.in
  www.southdelhipolytechnic.in/

- **State Institute for Development of Arts and Crafts (SIDAC, Odisha)**
  Bhubaneshwar, OD
  T: +91 674 2350298/2350310/2350318/2351389/6573705
  E: sidacorissa@gmail.com
  www.sidacodisha.org.in/

- **Textile Sector Skill India**
  New Delhi, DL
  E: contact@nationalskillsnetwork.com
  www.texskill.in/

- **Trifed**
  New Delhi, DL
  T: +91 11 26569064/26968247
  E: trifed@rediffmail.com
  www.trifed.tribal.gov.in/

Crafts Associations and Organizations

- **Aalekh Art | Architecture**
  Bengaluru, KA
  T: +91 9844814482
  E: pooja@aalekh.co.in

- **Ahambhumika Swayam Sevi Sanstha**
  Bhopal, MP
  T: +91 98264 72718
  www.ahambhumika.org/

- **Akhil Bharat Gudigar Samaj**
  Sagar, KA
  T: +91 94480 14176
  E: admin@gudigars.com
  · gudigarsworld@gmail.com

- **All India Artisans and Craftworkers Welfare Association (AIACA)**
  New Delhi, DL
  T: +91 11 26277491/2492
  E: contact@aiacaonline.org

- **Ambedkar Hastashilp Vikas Yojana (AHVY)**
  Office of the Development Commissioner (Handicrafts)
  Ministry of Textiles, Government of India
  New Delhi, DL
  E: dchejs@nic.in

- **Anand Metal Works**
  T: +91 9418030668

- **Andhra Pradesh Handicrafts Development Corporation Limited**
  Vijayawada, AP
  T: +91 8662578099 ·
  +91 9849900935
  · +91 9849900937
  E: info@lepakshihandicrafts.gov.in

- **Anwesha Tribal Arts and Crafts**
  Bhubaneswar, OD
  T: +91 674 2557497
  E: anwesha2k@rediffmail.com

- **Artisan's Hut**
  Firozabad, UP
  T: +91 9837275800

- **Assam Cane**
  Bengaluru, KA
  T: +91 9986570020
  E: sales@assamcane.com
  · info@assamcane.com

- **Bal Mahila Kalyan Vikas Ashram**
  Katihuar, BR
  T: +91 9835221585
  E: bmkva@rediffmail.com

- **Bangla Natak**
  Kolkata, WB
  T: +91 33 40047483
  E: banglanatak@gmail.com
  www.banglanatak.com

- **Bhavani Weaves Co-Operative**
  Chennai, TN
  E: bhavantex@gmail.com

- **Bhil Art**
  Industrial Design Centre, IIT Bombay
  Mumbai, MH
  T: +91 22 25767812
  E: ninamsabnani@iitb.ac.in
  www.bhilart.com/

- **Black Pottery Foundation**
  Azamgarh, UP
  E: sanjayyadav6340@gmail.com

- **Brahmaputra Fables**
  Guwahati, AS
  T: +91 8638059258
  E: brahmaputrafables@gmail.com

- **Centre for Cultural Studies and Research**
  Varanasi, UP
  T: +91 542 2366326
  jnanapravaha.vns@gmail.com

- **Centre for Social Reseach and Development**
  Guwahati, AS
  T: +91 9854031735 ·
  +91 361 2451549
  E: erpankajp@gmail.com

- **Coir Kerala**
  Alappuzha, KL
  T: +91 8281972684
  E: info@coirkerala.net ·
  jp@coirkerala.net

- **Council of Handicrafts Development Corporations**
  New Delhi, DL
  T: +91 11 26174198
  E: cohands@rediffmail.com
  · cohands83@gmail.com
  www.cohands.in

- **Craft Cluster of India**
  TN
  www.craftclustersofindia.in/
  site/Cluster_Directory.aspx?mu_
  id=3&idstate=24

- **Craftisan**
  New Delhi, DL
  T: +91 11 46551818

- **Craftizen**
  Bengaluru, KA
  T: +91 80 4814 0715 ·
  +91 9606071227
  E: connect@craftizen.org

- **CTok—Commitment to Kashmir**
  New Delhi, DL
  T: +91 9810327400 ·
  +91 9810603139
  E: ctok.dl@gmail.com

- **D'Source**
  Mumbai, MH
  T: +91 22 25767820/7801/7802
  E: dsource.in@gmail.com

- **Dastkar**
  New Delhi, DL
  +91 11 2680 8633 ·
  +91 9910802970

- **Dastkari Haat Samiti**
  New Delhi, DL
  T: +91 11 46084883
  www.dastkarihaat.org/

- **Decorcera**
  Gurugram, HR
  T: +91 8285644444 ·
  +91 124 432 0214
  www.decorcera.com/

- **Dehaati Design Studio**
  Kutch, GJ
  T: +91 9712955081 ·
  +91 9586855083
  E: info@dehaati.in ·
  dehaatidesign@gmail.com

- **Delhi Crafts Council**
  New Delhi, DL
  T: +91 11 26491571

- **Delhi Crafts Council**
  New Delhi, DL
  T: +91 11 26491571/49055415
  E: delhicraft@gmail.com

- **Department of Handicrafts, Jammu & Kashmir**
  Directorate of Handicrafts
  Srinagar, JK
  T: +91 194 2472065
  (From May to October)
  E: dir.handicraft@jk.gov.in
  Jammu, JK
  T: +91 191 2475536
  (From November to April)
  www.jkhandicrafts.com/index.htm

- **Dwarka Plus**
  Bengaluru, KA
  T: +91 80 4153 2087

- **Engrave**
  Mumbai, MH
  T: +91 7666122288
  E: support@engrave.in
  www.engrave.in/

- **Gaatha**
  Ahmedabad, GJ
  T: +91 79 26671008
  E: info@gaatha.com

- **Gem and Jewellery Skill Council of India**
  Mumbai, MH
  T: +91 22 28293942 ·
  +91 22 28293940/41/43

- **Golkonda Handicrafts Emporium**
  Hyderabad, TG
  T: +91 40 23235028 ·
  +91 40 23212902
  · +91 9908016678

- **Gramin Vikas Seva Sansthan**
  Mumbai, MH
  T: +91 9936012878
  E: gvss007@gmail.com

- **Handicrafts Development Corporation of Kerala**
  Trivandrum, KL
  T: +91 471 2331358/2778400
  E: hdckcw@gmail.com

- **Himalayan Environmental Studies And Conservation Organisation (HESCO)**
  New Delhi, DL
  T: +91 11 26590355
  E: ddutta@nic.in

- **Hiralaxmi Memorial Craft Park**
  Kutch, GJ
  T: +91 2832 240495/240496
  E: info@hmcraftpark.com

- **Indira Gandhi Rashtriya Manav Sangrahalaya**
  Bhopal, MP
  T: +91 7552661458
  www.igrms.com

- **INTACH, Jammu and Kashmir**
  Srinagar, JK
  E: intach.jk@gmail.com
  • intach.kashmir@gmail.com

- **Jagran Josh**
  New Delhi, DL
  T: +91 11 43093450
  E: contact@jagranjosh.com

- **Jaipur Rugs Foundation**
  Jaipur, RJ
  T: +91 141 3987400 •
  +91 141 7103400
  E: jrfoundation@jaipurrugs.org

- **Karnataka Handicrafts Development Corporation (KHDC)**
  Bengaluru, KA
  T: +91 7411118554 •
  +91 9448050935
  • +91 80 25581118
  E: sales@cauveryhandicrafts.net

- **Khamir**
  Kutch, GJ
  T: +91 2832 271272/422
  www.khamir.org/home

- **Kodungallur Thzhapaya Weavers Indl. Co–Op Society**
  Trichur, KL

- **Kottapuram Integrated Development Society (KIDS)**
  Trichur, KL
  T: +91 480 2803165/2807638
  • +91 9961204199
  E: kidskottapuram@gmail.com

- **Kraft Collective**
  Pune, MH
  T: +91 9604699966

- **Live History India**
  Mumbai MH
  E: contactus@livehistoryindia.com

- **Madras Makers Home Work Living**
  Chennai, TN
  T: +91 9176590085
  E: info@madrasmakers.com
  www.madrasmakers.com/

- **MeMeraki**
  Gurugram, HR
  T: +91 9971593574
  E: wecare@memeraki.com

- **Mianzi**
  New Delhi, DL
  T: +91 7738692900
  E: contactus@mianzi.in

- **MITHILAsmita Art & Craft**
  New Delhi, DL
  T: +91 9901187800
  E: sales@mithilasmita.com

- **Mizo Heritage**
  Aizawl, MZ
  T: +91 9436154391
  https://aizawl.nic.in/handicraft-2/

- **Molela Terracotta Handicrafts Producer Company Limited**
  Udaipur, RJ

- **Nilambar Terracotta and Murals**
  T: +91 9747622922

- **Obsidianspace**
  Bhopal, MP
  E: obsidianspaceblog@gmail.com

- **ODOPUP**
  Lucknow, UP
  T: +91 522 2616313 •
  +91 9415467934
  • +91 7234805011
  E: odopcell@gmail.com
  www.odopup.in

- **Omkar Arts & Crafts Association**
  Marcela, GA
  T: +91 9326117670
  E: omkaranc@rediffmail.com

- **w Rural and Urban Producers' Association (ORUPA)**
  Bhubaneswar, OD
  T: +91 674 2563706

- **P-TAL Punjab Thathera Art Legacy**
  Amritsar, PB
  T: +91 9669631316 •
  +91 7428735295 • +91 8093858157
  E: aditya.agrawal@p-tal.org
  www.p-tal.org • www.ptal.in

- **P. O. Mahendramangalam**
  Tiruchilapalli, TN
  https://www.khadi.com/

- **Panchmura Mrit Shilpi Samabay Samity (Union)**
  Kolkata, WB
  T: +91 33 40047482/83 •
  +91 8420106396/8
  toureast@banglanatak.com

- **Paramparik Karigar**
  T: +91 9152493658
  www.paramparikkarigar.com/

- **Peepul Tree**
  T: +91 8169937689
  E: support@peepultree.in

- **Poompuhar, Tamil Nadu Handicrafts**
  Chennai, TN
  T: +91 44 28521271 •
  +91 44 28521798
  E: tamilnaduhandicrafts@yahoo.co.in

- **Pratibha Art**
  Raipur, CT
  T: +91 7828047105
  E: support@pratibhaart.com
  www.pratibhaart.com

- **Raah Foundation**
  Mumbai, MH
  T: +91 22 24448082 •
  +91 9869423122
  E: info@raahfoundation.org

- **Rainbow Textiles**
  GJ
  T: +91 9825849650 •
  +91 9428896230
  E: shakil.khatri.2009@gmail.com

- **Sabala Heritage Home**
  Bijapur, KA
  T: +91 9448118204
  E: sabalaheritagehome@gmail.com

- **Sahayog**
  Bidar, KA
  T: +91 8482 236147 •
  +91 9845980912
  E: info@sahayogbidar.org

- **Saif Faisal Design Workshop**
  T: +91 7829820809
  E: design@saif-faisal.com
  www.saif-faisal.com/

- **Sakoya Foundation**
  Maujpur, DL
  T: +91 9654478368 •
  +91 9654478368
  E: sakoyafoundation@gmail.com

- **Sampoorna Bamboo Kendra**
  Amravati, MH
  T: +91 7226202370 •
  +91 9421825925 • +91 9421825970
  E: sampoornabamboo@gmail.com

- **Samta Foundation**
  Mumbai, MH
  T: +91 22 67733650 •
  +91 7517868686
  E: samta@samtafoundation.org

- **Sanatkada**
  Lucknow, UP
  T: +91 7080701510
  E: sanatkada@gmail.com

- **Sarath Etikoppaka Toys**
  Etikoppaka, AP
  T: +91 9533953639
  E: hello@etikoppakatoys.com

- **Sargaalaya Kerala Arts and Crafts Village**
  Kozhikode, KL
  T: +91 496 2606015 •
  +91 9446309222
  E: sargaalaya@gmail.com
  www.sargaalaya.in/

- **Self Employed Women's Association (SEWA)**
  Ahmedabad, GJ
  T: +91 79 25506444 •
  +91 79 25506477

- **Shakti Kachhi Mud and Mirror-work**
  Kutch, GJ
  T: +91 9638658014 •
  +91 7016135758

- **Shatabdi Craft & Social Welfare Society**
  Dewas, MP
  E: sandeeproy1966@gmail.com
  www.shatabdicrafts.com

- **Shri Sai Black Potri**
  Azamgarh, UP
  T: +91 7071336241

- **Silver Linings**
  T: +91 7331176568
  E: info@silverlinings.in

Crafts Associations and Organizations • 257

Crafts Associations and Organizations

- **Studio Coppre**
  Pune, MH
  T: +91 9168978684
  E: hello@coppre.in

- **Studio Renesa**
  New Delhi, DL
  T: +91 11 45511211/ 457 00 411
  E: renesa91@gmail.com

- **Tara Books**
  Chennai, TN
  T: +91 9150323115

- **Tarkashi**
  Mumbai, MH
  T: +91 8104739048
  E: info@tarkashi.co.in
  www.tarkashi.co.in/Home/contact

- **TFOD Lifestyles Pvt. Ltd.**
  Mumbai, MH
  T: +91 9930350555
  E: support@tfod.in

- **The Art Centrix Space**
  New Delhi, DL
  T: +91 9811040289
  E: artcentrixspace@gmail.com
  info@artcentrix.com

- **The Artisan Foundation**
  Mumbai, MH
  T: +91 7045423944
  E: theartisanfoundation@gmail.com

- **The Chamunda Handloom and Handicraft Co-operative Industrial Society Limited**
  Kangra, HP
  T: +91 9868512321

- **The Craft Council of Haryana**
  Faridabad, HR
  E: cchr@rediffmail.com

- **The Crafts Council of Karnataka**
  T: +91 80 23462520
  E: info@thecraftscouncilofkarnataka.org

- **The Hans India**
  Hyderabad, TG
  T: +91 40 23730070

- **The Kailash Handloom & Handicraft Production Co-op Industrial Society Ltd.**
  Kullu, HP

- **Tata Shilp Kala Sansthan**
  Chamba, HP

- **The M.Rm.Rm Cultural Foundation**
  Chennai, TN
  T: +91 6374627663 •
  +91 44 24622505/ 24614313

- **Tripura Bamboo And Cane Development Centre**
  Ghaziabad, DL
  T: +91 8800947095
  E: info@cibart.in

- **Tripura Bamboo Mission Government of Tripura**
  Agartala, TR
  T: +91 9862427467 •
  +91 9862972164 • +91 9436995131
  E: tripurabamboo@gmail.com

- **Tvami**
  Bengaluru, KA
  T: +91 6364003940
  E: support@tvami.com

- **Urbanhut Vernaculars**
  Dhatir Palwal, HR
  T: +91 9910514460

- **Varnam**
  Bengaluru, KA
  T: +91 80 25250360/41200189
  • +91 9980735911
  E: myvarnam@gmail.com

- **Vikaspedia, India Development Gateway (InDG) Initiative**
  Hyderabad, TG
  E: indg@cdac.in

- **Wonky Works**
  Vadodara, GJ
  T: +91 9426789935
  E: hi@wonkyworks.in

- **Youth Club of Bejjipuram (YCB)**
  Srikakulam, AP
  T: +91 894 2279305 • +91 9490162667
  E: youthclubofbejjipuram@gmail.com
  • youthclubofbejjipuram@yahoo.co.in
  www.ycbindia.org

Principal Committee 2019-2021

(Institute of Indian Interior Designers)

Jabeen Zacharias
National President, IIID

Aparna Bidarkar
NEC Member and Chairperson,
Hyderabad Chapter, IIID

Principal Architect,
Hue Designs

Rajeev Sathe
Architect

Ayush Kasliwal
Creative Director,
AKFD/AnanTaya

Jignesh Modi
National Honorary
Secretary, IIID

Chairman, Indian Institute
of Architects, Surat Center

Contributors

Advisory Committee

Aman Nath is a historian by education. A founder-member of INTACH, he has been actively involved in the restoration of India's lesser-known architectural ruins, and is the Co-founder of Neemrana Hotels, which were nominated in 2004 for the Aga Khan Award, and have won awards from UNESCO, the Indian travel trade industry, as well as National Awards from the Government of India. He is also the author of several books, among them *Arts and Crafts of Rajasthan*, with the late Francis Wacziarg (Mapin, 1997). He was recently honoured with the Condé Nast Lifetime Achievement Award, 2017.

Jaya Jaitly has worked closely with India's craftspeople to preserve traditional craft livelihoods and cultural heritage since 1967. A leader and expert in the field of craft studies, she is the Founder and President of Dastkari Haat Samiti, a national association of Indian craftspeople, which she set up in 1986. She also established Dilli Haat, a permanent and now iconic crafts marketplace in New Delhi, in 1994. She recently collaborated with Google and the Ministry of Tourism to create "Crafted in India," the largest online exposition of craft stories, in 2019. She is the author of *Crafts of Jammu, Kashmir and Ladakh* (Mapin, 1999) and the seminal *Crafts Atlas of India*, among many others. Her latest work is *Life Among the Scorpions: A Memoir of a Woman in Indian Politics*.

Parul Zaveri established Abhikram (Sanskrit for "initiation") with the late Nimish Patel in 1979 with a view to making design more balanced, contextual and functional for the end-user. Having studied at CEPT, Ahmedabad and the Massachusetts Institute of Technology in the United States of America, she worked with the visionary architect Paolo Soleri in Arizona, and in Nigeria, before returning to India in 1979. Ever since, for more than four decades, Abhikram has pursued responsible architecture, focusing on energy conservation and establishing the relevance of traditional materials, processes and crafts in contemporary designs. Their works have received national and international acclaim for conservation and adaptive reuse of built structures, as well as for their passive-cooled and contemporary buildings. She is a visiting faculty at CEPT, Ahmedabad and the National Institute of Design, Ahmedabad.

A. Balasubramaniam is a product designer based in Gurgaon, India. He is the Founder of January Design, a design consultancy that works mainly with marginal crafts, grass-roots innovations and the MSME sectors of the industry. An early graduate of the National Institute of Design, Ahmedabad, he is currently the Director of the Institute of Design at J.K. Lakshmipat University, Jaipur. He regularly writes on design issues in major publications, as well as his own blog, *Design Thoughts*.

Arjun Rathi is an architect and lighting designer and the Founder of Arjun Rathi Design. Established in 2011, his work has gained national and international recognition for its exploratory approach to design processes.

Asha Sairam is a Design Principal at Studio Lotus. Part of this pioneering studio since 2010, she heads teams in articulating brands to the built environment from concept to detail and uses her diverse experience across verticals to shape definitive projects at the practice.

Ayush Kasliwal is the Creative Director and Co-founder of AKFD and Anantaya, based in Jaipur, India. Their works have been recognized through several awards, including the LEXUS Design Award 2019; AD 100; the Kyoorius Design Award 2019; and the EDIDA award 2018, 2017, 2013.

Kristine Michael is a ceramic artist, curator and writer based in New Delhi. She is also an arts educator and currently holds the position of Curriculum Leader of Visual and Dramatic Arts at The British School in New Delhi. She was most recently a contributor to the book *Mutable: Ceramic and Clay Art in India Since 1947* (Mapin, 2021).

Mitchell Abdul Karim Crites has spent his life studying, preserving and reviving the great art forms of the Islamic world. He is the author of the best-selling *India Sublime* among others. His current projects include the world's longest monumental calligraphic marble panels, inlaid with lapis lazuli, for the important Al-Shamiya Extension project in Mecca Sharif.

Neelam Chhiber, an award-winning social entrepreneur, is Co-founder and Managing Trustee at Industree Crafts Foundation. An Industrial Design graduate from NID, Ahmedabad, she has for the past three decades been working with artisans in rural areas, by providing design, technical, marketing and management solutions to bridge the urban-rural chasm.

Rebecca Reubens works at the intersection of design, craft and sustainability. Her PhD at the Delft University of Technology focused on the links between sustainability, design, craft and development. She is the author of the books *Bamboo: From Green Design to Sustainable Design*, and *Holistic Sustainability Through Craft-Design Collaboration*.

First published in 2023 by
Mapin Publishing Pvt. Ltd
706 Kaivanna,
Panchvati, Ellisbridge,
Ahmedabad 380006
Gujarat, India

and

Institute of Indian Interior Designers (IIID)
109 Sumer Kendra
Pandurang Budhkar Marg
Worli, Mumbai 400018
Maharashtra, India

© Institute of Indian Interior Designers (IIID) and
Mapin Publishing, 2021
All rights reserved.

Text © Authors
Photographs © as listed
For all individual entries from designers/design
studios, photographs have been reproduced with
permission from the respective entries.

The moral rights of Jaya Jaitly, Aman Nath,
Asha Sairam, Kristine Michael, Neelam Chhiber,
Rebecca Reubens, A. Balasubramaniam,
Mitchell Abdul Karim Crites, Ayush Kasliwal and
Arjun Rathi as authors of this work are asserted.

ISBN: 978-93-85360-94-7

Copyediting: Mithila Rangarajan / Mapin Editorial
Proofreading: Ateendriya Gupta,
 Neha Manke / Mapin Editorial
Design: Gopal Limbad / Mapin Design Studio
Production: Mapin Design Studio
Printed in China

CAPTIONS

FRONT COVER: The reception area for a Delhi-based office features a vivid backdrop of paper cutouts of Delhi's architectural landmarks and fauna. These were executed by master craftsman Ram Soni using the delicate but impactful *sanjhi* technique, in association with artisans from Dastkari Haat Samiti. (See pp. 76–77)

PAGE 1: A partition wall in *jali* style made of locally-sourced laterite and khondalite (sandstone) at Krushi Bhawan in Bhubaneswar. (See pp. 30–31)

PAGES 2–3: Canopy made of jute ropes provides a way to manipulate sunlight and air at this rooftop cafe in Ahmedabad. (See pp. 74–75)

PAGES 4–5: A suite at the Tijara Fort heritage hotel features a large frescoed wall along with the decor in the seating area bringing in the *mela* atmosphere of a village fair. (See pp. 212–217)

PAGE 6: An accent wall created using *lippan kaam* and *aabhla* work at a residence in Gujarat. (See pp. 164–165)

BACK COVER: This stunning, unusual hanging lamp, designed by Ankon Mitra and Neha Bhardwaj, is made of hand-folded parchment leather and knitted wool. It brings together Indian and Japanese craft techniques to create a product that uses traditional materials within a modern design. (See pp. 140–141)